ROUTLEDGE LIBRARY EDITIONS:
SHAKESPEARE IN PERFORMANCE

Volume 5

TRANSLATION, POETICS, AND THE STAGE

TRANSLATION, POETICS, AND THE STAGE
Six French *Hamlets*

ROMY HEYLEN

Routledge
Taylor & Francis Group
LONDON AND NEW YORK

First published in 1993

This edition first published in 2014
by Routledge
2 Park Square, Milton Park, Abingdon, Oxon, OX14 4RN

and by Routledge
711 Third Avenue, New York, NY 10017

Routledge is an imprint of the Taylor & Francis Group, an informa business

© 1993 Romy Heylen

All rights reserved. No part of this book may be reprinted or reproduced or utilised in any form or by any electronic, mechanical, or other means, now known or hereafter invented, including photocopying and recording, or in any information storage or retrieval system, without permission in writing from the publishers.

Trademark notice: Product or corporate names may be trademarks or registered trademarks, and are used only for identification and explanation without intent to infringe.

British Library Cataloguing in Publication Data
A catalogue record for this book is available from the British Library

ISBN: 978-1-138-78774-2 (Set)
eISBN: 978-1-315-76168-8 (Set)
ISBN: 978-1-138-79086-5 (Volume 5)
eISBN: 978-1-315-76397-2 (Volume 5)

Publisher's Note
The publisher has gone to great lengths to ensure the quality of this book but points out that some imperfections from the original may be apparent.

Disclaimer
The publisher has made every effort to trace copyright holders and would welcome correspondence from those they have been unable to trace.

Translation, Poetics, and the Stage

Six French *Hamlets*

Romy Heylen

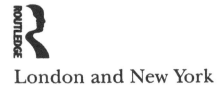
London and New York

First published 1993
by Routledge
11 New Fetter Lane, London EC4P 4EE

Simultaneously published in the USA and Canada
by Routledge
29 West 35th Street, New York, NY 10001

© 1993 Romy Heylen

Typeset in 10/12pt Baskerville by
Ponting–Green Publishing Services, Sunninghill, Berkshire
Printed in Great Britain by
T J Press (Padstow) Ltd, Padstow, Cornwall

All rights reserved. No part of this book may be reprinted
or reproduced or utilized in any form or by any electronic,
mechanical, or other means, now known or hereafter
invented, including photocopying and recording, or in any
information storage or retrieval system, without permission
in writing from the publishers.

British Library Cataloguing in Publication Data

A catalogue record for this book is available from
the British Library

Library of Congress Cataloging in Publication Data
Heylen, Romy,
    Translation, poetics, and the stage / Romy Heylen.
      p. cm. – (Translation studies)
    Includes bibliographical references and index.
    1. Shakespeare, William, 1564–1616 – Hamlet.
    2. Shakespeare, William, 1564–1616 – Translations
into French – History and criticism. 3. Shakespeare,
William, 1564–1616 – Stage history – France. 4. English
language – Translating into French – History.
5. Drama – Translations – History and criticism. 6.
Translating and interpreting – History. 7. Poetics.
I. Title. II. Series: Translation Studies
(London, England)
    PR2807.H48 1993
    822.3'3–dc20   92-11713

ISBN 0–415–07689–7

Voor Sjoeki

Contents

Acknowledgments	x
Introduction: A cultural model of translation	1
1 **Jean-François Ducis'** *Hamlet, Tragédie imitée de l'anglois* A neoclassical tragedy?	26
2 **Alexandre Dumas and Paul Meurice's** *Hamlet, Prince de Danemark* Translation as an exercise in power	45
3 **Marcel Schwob and Eugène Morand's** *La Tragique Histoire d'Hamlet* A folkloric prose translation	61
4 **The blank verse shall halt for't** André Gide's *La Tragédie d'Hamlet*	77
5 **Yves Bonnefoy's** *La Tragédie d'Hamlet* An allegorical translation	92
6 **Theatre as translation/Translation as theatre** *Shakespeare's Hamlet* by the Théâtre du Miroir	122
Concluding remarks	137
Appendix: Table of selected *Hamlet* **productions**	140
Notes	146
Index	165

Acknowledgments

I would like to express my heartfelt thanks to those people without whose help I would not have been able to finish this book. Firstly I am deeply indebted to both André Lefevere and Susan Bassnett for having had the patience and the understanding to see this project through from beginning to end. Their constant support and encouragement has helped to sustain my interest in Translation Studies, and hopefully this series will do the same for others. Thanks are also due to Jean-Michel Déprats for his kindness in granting me access to material that would otherwise have remained inaccessible to me. His help in answering questions of a technical nature on the various productions of *Hamlet*, especially those involving the Théâtre du Miroir, made my task immeasurably easier. Next I am grateful to Amy Baskin, Laura Johnson and Shira Schwam-Baird whose willingness to type around the clock went above and beyond the call of duty. Finally, I wish to express my gratitude to Andrew Henstock for keeping me in coffee and sane throughout the writing and rewriting of this book.

Extracts from chapter 5 have appeared in *The French Review*, vol. 66, no. 2, 1992; and in *Comparative Literature Studies*, vol. 29, no. 4, 1992.

Introduction: A cultural model of translation

The development of translation studies as an academic field evolved from the work of the Russian linguist Andrei Fedorov and the American Eugene A. Nida who, using the insights of linguistics and the findings of logic, semantics, information and communications theory, discovered in translation certain regularities which they described in the form of theoretical statements. Subsequently, the study of translation came to be considered as one of two special branches of linguistics: either as applied or as comparative or contrastive linguistics. Yet the validity of the incorporation of translation studies exclusively into the discipline of linguistics is questionable. Translation theorists have pointed out that this integration only occurred in the first place due to a confusion of the field of study with the method of study.[1] Literary scholars and social scientists could likewise have annexed the investigation of translations and translating, respectively. Whereas in the past literary scholars, especially comparatists, seldom concerned themselves with translations as instruments of mediation and influence between national literatures, there has lately been a growing interest in the phenomenon of translation. The shift of attention in literary studies to considerations of the impact, reception, and communicative function of a literary work of art has acted as the motivating factor behind the study of literary translations and the role they play in the literary process.[2]

In recent years, the field of translation studies has become a relatively independent discipline with clearly delineated goals, i.e. the description of translations and translation processes and the discovery of general rules for the development of models capable of explaining these phenomena.[3] In addition to this descriptive and theoretical aspect, translation studies as an academic discipline involves the development of lexicographical, contrastive-grammatical, and comparative stylistic tools, translation criticism, and translation training.

Translation has traditionally been accorded a low academic status, since it was considered to be a secondary or derivative activity whose very existence depended on other primary or "original" text production.[4] The comparison of translations with original works inevitably resulted in the evaluation of translations in terms of "right" and "wrong." The main objective critics had was to find fault with the translator and to pinpoint "mistakes" in the translation. The assumption was that all translations were in some way destined to fail the original, neatly reducing the critics' task to that of deciding whether or not a translation was "faithful" to the original text. Such an ideal was and is based on the principle of complete "equivalence," which is thought to ensure the accuracy of a translation. The conditions for equivalence are postulates of normative and absolute theories concerned with the problem of translatability. They imply a mechanical transfer of translation units or certain fixed data. While such normative, or prescriptive theories find a ready-made application in the research for machine translation, concerned with contemporary texts which contain technical information, they are not ideally suited to the analysis of literary translations.

Prescriptive theories of translation, at least in the English-speaking world, have their roots in the eighteenth century. Alexander Tytler's *Essay on the Principles of Translation* (1791) is generally considered to be the first theoretical essay on the subject in English.[5] Tytler introduces his essay with a description of a "good translation" and establishes the "general rules" derived from that description.[6] Although it attempts to be a systematic study of the translation process in English, Tytler's essay is essentially a manual for eighteenth-century professional and amateur translators. The general, prescriptive rules are: (1) the translation should give a complete transcript of the ideas of the original work; (2) the style and manner of writing should be of the same character as that of the original; (3) the translation should read with all the ease and fluency of the original composition.[7] These "laws" are abundantly illustrated. Tytler's essay offers a blueprint, examples, and several translation rules for eighteenth-century translators. His essay belongs to what today would be called applied translation studies and reflects eighteenth-century translation poetics.

However, most theories on translation, not just Tytler's, have been normative. The norms contained in these theories consist of the authors' personal, national, and time-bound values, which they have elevated to the status of general and universal rules. A more recent example of such a normative translation theory can be found in Eugene A. Nida and Charles R. Taber's *The Theory and Practice of Translation*.[8] Their guidebook for what should be done in specific instances of translation establishes

> certain fundamental sets of priorities: (1) contextual consistency has priority over verbal consistency (or word-for-word concordance), (2) dynamic equivalence has priority over formal correspondence, (3) the aural (heard) form of language has priority over the written form, (4) forms that are used by and acceptable to the audience for which a translation is intended have priority over forms that may be traditionally more prestigious.[9]

This "system of priorities" constitutes a normative theory which presents itself as a general theory of translation, although it is actually designed for a particular kind of text (the Bible), to help out a particular kind of translator (the modern Bible translator), and adheres to a particular notion of how the Bible should be read (aloud in worship services rather than, say, silently in one's home). These prescriptive theories of translation set out to discuss translation problems specific to certain texts, but very soon they prescribe what translation in general *should be*, and then develop a taxonomy of rules and laws for all translations.

Most contemporary theories of translation could be called prescriptive. This is partly due to the hybrid role of translation, which is both a technique for teaching and learning a foreign language, and an exercise to be taught and learned in itself. Translations rendered by students need to be judged according to certain criteria. Future professional translators are expected to produce reliable interpretations, and they have to be evaluated by their teachers. Critics who review published translations are asked to offer an informative judgment on the performance of the translator or on the translation's value.[10] All these activities occur within a prescriptive framework.

Those who advocate normative approaches to translation have traditionally been insensitive to certain socio-cultural aspects which play an important role in the translation process. They reduce the problem of translation to the problem of translatability and ignore the conditions under which translations are produced so that they may function in the receiving culture. In reality, however, the conditions required to produce "equivalence" differ from period to period, and from language culture to language culture. A text which functions as a translation today may not be called a "translation" tomorrow and may be named a "version" instead; a translation strategy (turning verse into prose) which was valid in the past may not be seen to be the most effective strategy of reflecting the original today. Historical changes and the socio-cultural context of the reception of translation determine a reader's expectations, and form part of his or her notion of what constitutes translation.

Jean-François Ducis translated Shakespeare's *Hamlet* into alexandrines and the play subsequently became the most frequently produced eighteenth-century drama at the Comédie Française after the works of Voltaire.[11] Marcel Schwob and Eugène Morand, 130 years later, translated the play into an artificially created seventeenth-century French prose, which was hailed by contemporary critics as daring and innovative, and performed by Sarah Bernhardt to packed houses in 1899.[12] Normative theorists would simply regard such translations as horrible mistakes. Since they are concerned with the evaluation of translations only on the basis of their own pre-established criteria, they can only tell us whether they are "good" or "bad" according to their own time-bound rules. Normative approaches offer no insight into the specific rationale behind certain translation practices, such as those behind the Ducis and the Schwob-Morand translations of *Hamlet*. Paying attention to historical and cultural constraints on translation, however, makes us more aware of the reasons behind a translator's decisions. A historically descriptive translation model can account for such "non-equivalent" efforts as those of Ducis and Schwob-Morand and will lead discussions away from normative notions of "right" and "wrong." At the end of the eighteenth century, Shakespeare's blank verse was an unfamiliar poetic form for French readers. In order to appropriate *Hamlet* and to make the play accessible to French readers and spectators, Ducis decided to make use of a form to which they were accustomed. At the end of the nineteenth century Schwob and Morand sought to make the play produce the same reaction (in terms of its poetic and dramatic effect) in French readers and spectators as in their English counterparts, by grounding the play in French folklore. These examples demonstrate that translation can be a goal-oriented socio-cultural activity. Other translators, from different cultures and different time periods, will render *Hamlet* differently, not because they are making mistakes, but because they are working under different socio-historical and cultural constraints. Hence, in order to explain the time- and culture-bound criteria which play an important role in the translator's activity, a non-prescriptive translation model is essential. A descriptive, historical model of translation goes beyond questions of whether and to what degree a translation matches an original; it investigates the underlying constraints and motivations which inform the translation process. Translation is a teleological activity of a profoundly transformative nature. Therefore, normative models of translation based on the absolute concept of equivalence need to be replaced by a historical-relative and socio-cultural model of translation.

The proposal of a framework for such a cultural model of translation is necessarily beholden to a number of concepts developed by individual translation theorists whose work has taken them toward the advocation of a basically functional, socio-culturally rooted framework for the study of translation. Itamar Even-Zohar, for example, introduces the idea of the polysystem; Gideon Toury adds the important notion of translational norms; James S. Holmes refers to his conception of the "translator's map" and also includes the notion of shifts in his analysis of the translation process. Jiří Levý, meanwhile, posits a framework based on a view of translation as a rebus which the translator must solve by means of a teleological decision-making process, necessarily involving shifts. For Lawrence Venuti, translation is largely a code-abiding process within the context of capitalist society, as opposed to Barbara Harlow, for whom the process of translation is a strategy of cultural resistance within the framework of deconstruction and decolonization. Finally, the outline for the cultural model of translation proposed here is indebted to André Lefevere's notion of translation as a form of rewriting which in turn makes use of Fredric Jameson's concept of the master code as a means of interpreting the translation of texts as an exercise in manipulation.

Itamar Even-Zohar's collection of essays, *Papers in Historical Poetics*, introduces the idea of literature and translated literature as a polysystem.[13] His approach is based on the working hypothesis that it is more convenient to take all sorts of literary and semi-literary texts as an aggregate of systems, a heterogeneous system of systems, or a polysystem. Even-Zohar first posited the concept of the literary polysystem in 1970 in order to study the relationship between different kinds of texts: "great" literary works, popular literature, translations, etc. His approach is deeply rooted in the structuralist and semiotic traditions of the Russian Formalists and Czech Structuralists.

Even-Zohar focuses on the relationships between various types of literature and their synchronic and diachronic interaction. He observes that the part played by translations in a literature is inherently connected with the historical evolution of that literature. Every literary system necessarily exists as an evolution and this evolution is inescapably of a systemic nature. This means that the opposition between the synchronic and diachronic study of literature loses its importance in principle. Averse to translation studies which treat "translated works" as individual units in isolation from other texts, Even-Zohar argues for the study of translation in terms of "historical functions." In other words, individual literary translations and their intrinsic meaning are no longer considered a relevant object for literary studies. Instead, Even-Zohar encourages the investigation of translations in their systemic relationship with the surrounding literary polysystem. This theory conceives of literature as a stratified whole, itself a polysystem whose main components are "canonized" as opposed to "non-canonized" literature, each consisting in its turn of separate sub-systems or genres. The term "canonized literature" roughly indicates what is generally considered major literature: those kinds of literary works accepted by the literary milieu and usually preserved by the community as part of its cultural heritage. "Non-canonized literature" refers to those kinds of literary works which are usually rejected by the literary milieu as lacking in "aesthetic value." Even-Zohar recognizes that canonization is not a simple notion; the dichotomy he refers to also denotes the tension between official and unofficial cultural strata. The intra-systemic relationships within a polysystem are ultimately constrained by a larger socio-cultural system. Many components of this mechanism have been transformed into functions operating within co-systems "closer" to the literary polysystem; sub-divisions of "literary life," for example literary institutions such as publishing houses, periodicals, critical works, and other mediating factors, often channel the "more remote" constraints of the socio-cultural system. Literary stratification does not operate on the level of "texts" alone, nor are texts stratified exclusively according to features inherent in them. Rather, the constraints imposed upon the "literary" polysystem by its various semiotic co-systems (religious, political, socio-economic, etc.) contribute their share to the hierarchical relationships which govern it.

The various literary systems and types maintain hierarchical relationships: some occupy a more central position than others, or some are "primary" while others are "secondary." "Primary" activity is presumed to be that activity which takes the initiative when it comes to the creation of new items and models in literature; it represents the principle of innovation. "Secondary" activity, on the other hand, is conceived of as a derivative and conservative activity; it represents the principle which conforms to established norms and codes.

Translated literature must be included in the literary polysystem in order that its interaction with other literary systems may be studied. Whether translated literature becomes primary or secondary depends, according to Even-Zohar, upon the specific circumstances operating within the polysystem. As long as it maintains a primary function, translated literature participates actively in shaping the center of the polysystem. This situation often results in the blurring of any clear-cut distinction between original and translated writings. Perceived as such, translations are likely to become one of the ways of elaborating new models and will form an integral part of innovative forces in the receiving culture. Even-Zohar distinguishes three major historical moments in which translated literature may acquire a primary position: (1) when a polysystem has not yet been crystallized (i.e. when a literature is "young," for instance, or in the process of being established); (2) when a literature is either "peripheral" or "weak" or both; (3) when there are turning points, crises, or "literary vacuums" in a literature. At any of these moments translated literature may assume a primary position within a literary polysystem. However, if translated literature occupies a secondary position, it cannot influence the canonization of works in the receiving literature and will be modeled according to norms already conventionally established; in such cases it operates as a major force for the preservation of the receiving cultural norms and models. The conditions under which translated literature assumes a secondary position indicate either that there are no major changes in the polysystem or that these changes are not brought about through the intervention of interliterary relations manifest in the form of translation.

The hypothesis that translated literature may fall into either a primary or secondary category does not imply, however, that it is always wholly one or the other. As a system, translated literature is itself stratified, and it is from the vantage point of the central stratum that all other relations within the system are observed: while one section of translated literature may assume a primary position, another may remain secondary. The major clue to this issue, according to Even-Zohar, is the close relationship between literary contacts and the status of translated literature. Arguing against gratuitous "influence" studies, Even-Zohar suggests some universals of "literary contacts."[14] He also reminds us that not all polysystems are structured in the same way and that cultures do differ significantly, especially in their "openness" toward other literatures or in the flexibility with which they negotiate cultural differences.[15]

The position translated literature occupies at a given point in time also has its bearing on translational norms, the prevailing literary taste, and the policies of publishers and editors with regard to foreign material. The distinction between a translated work and an original work in terms of literary behavior, for instance, is, according to Even-Zohar, a clear function of the position assumed by translated literature at a certain time. When translated literature takes up a primary position, the borderlines between translated works and original works are diffuse. The translator's main concern in this case is not to look for ready-made models in the receiving literature; instead, he or she will be prepared to introduce new poetic models based on the form of the original text. Under such conditions, Even-Zohar claims, "the chances that a translation will be close to the original in terms of adequacy (in other words a reproduction of the dominant textual relations of the original) are greater than otherwise."[16] But when translated literature occupies a secondary position the translator's main effort will be to concentrate upon finding the best ready-made poetic models through which to represent the foreign text in the receiving literature. Here, Even-Zohar remarks that the result often turns out to be a "non-adequate translation"; there is "a greater discrepancy between the equivalence achieved and the adequacy postulated."[17] In short, not only is the socio-literary status of translation dependent upon its position within the receiving literary system; so is its very practice.

Seen from this point of view translation is not a phenomenon whose parameters are fixed once and for all, but an activity dependent on the relationships within a certain cultural system. Such key concepts as adequacy and equivalence cannot be dealt with fairly unless the implications of polysystemic positions are taken into account. According to Even-Zohar, neglect of these polysystemic positions is one of the major defects of contemporary translation theories which lean too heavily on "static linguistic models" or "undeveloped theories of literature."[18]

Although Even-Zohar's introduction of an opposition between "primary" and "secondary" positions has been justifiably criticized, it still provides a viable framework for the study of translation, and more specifically, for the study of translated literature.[19] The objection to thinking in terms of systems is that every system necessarily generates its own countersystem and that change or evolution are inherent features of any system. Consequently, no system needs to be devised to explain them. Every system necessarily exists as an evolution and the history of such a system itself becomes a system. The problem with Even-Zohar's thinking in terms of systems is that evolution is not always of a systemic nature. Moreover, although Even-Zohar stresses that the "primary versus secondary" opposition is a historical-typological notion, that very notion is conducive to evaluation since all texts are defined from the point of view of the "center" of the polysystem. The distinction between the primary and secondary position of translated literature could also be defined from the "periphery" of the polysystem, which – needless to say – would then entail a reversal in perspective and signification. However, Even-Zohar's theoretical framework remains useful for the development of a historical-relative, socio-cultural translation model in that it rejects normative approaches on the basis of their *a priori* and ahistorical conception of translation. His functionalist view of translated literature does not determine in advance what a translation is, or should be, or to what extent a translation has to correspond to an original; instead, it examines these questions from the standpoint of conditions operative in the receiving literature. The importance of an individual translation for the polysystem is determined only by the position it may have occupied in the process of innovation or preservation within a literary system. Consequently, when studying translations one should also analyze translation criticism, reflective essays on translation, prefaces to translations, or any material which expresses the commonly accepted "good" taste or the translational norms operating in a given literature at a certain moment in time.

Gideon Toury contributes yet another element to the study of translated literature which describes existing translations: the notion of translational norms. Supporting the polysystem hypothesis, he analyzes the nature and role of norms in literary translation in his book entitled *In Search of a Theory of Translation* and examines possible sources and methods for the study of these norms.[20] His notion of what constitutes a "norm" is based on the research of sociologists and social psychologists. Sociology regards norms as

> the translation of general values or ideas shared by a certain community – as to what is right and wrong, adequate and inadequate – into specific performance-instructions appropriate for and applicable to specific situations, providing they are not (yet) formulated as laws.[21]

Individual members of the community acquire, even internalize, these instructions or norms during the socialization process, and these norms then serve as criteria for the evaluation of actual instances of behavior. In other words, the norms to which Toury refers are not absolute, but socio-historical, and can be used to characterize the "horizon of expectation" of the translator and his or her receiving culture.[22]

The aforementioned translational norms are sub-divided into preliminary, initial, and operational categories. Preliminary norms relate to matters of selecting a text for translation, whereas the initial norm governs the basic choice a translator makes between adherence to the source text and concern for the prospective new reader. Operational norms concern actual decisions made in the process of translating. Here Toury differentiates between matricial norms, which determine the matrix of a translated text, and textual norms, which determine its actual formulation. This classification of norms could possibly be refined, but it serves the purpose of drawing our attention to the fact that choices and decisions are made at several levels of the translation process and, what is more, that the results of these choices can be detected in the translation product and can therefore be described with the help of Toury's model.

In his discussion of the initial norm, Toury explicitly mentions only its linguistic and literary aspects. Similarly, when he describes operational norms, Toury states that textual norms are either purely linguistic or purely literary. That is to say, he omits to outline the socio-cultural dimension of the text. In order to adopt Toury's notion of norms for the purposes of a cultural model it would be necessary to make his linguistic and literary norms part of an overall polysystem of cultural norms and codes.

Although Toury discusses translational norms in relation to the process of translating, his main focus is on what could be referred to as the "translation product," since he considers the product of translation to be more accessible to the analyst than the process by which it was produced. Consequently, Toury's notion of norm becomes a category for the descriptive analysis of translation phenomena. He recognizes two major sources for the study of translational norms: translated texts themselves and

> extratextual, semi-theoretical or critical formulations, such as prescriptive theories (or poetics) of translation, statements made by translators, editors, publishers, and other persons involved in or connected with translation, in public as well as

in private, critical appraisals of single translations, and so forth.[23]

Translated texts present analysts of translation with the results of actual norm-regulated behavior from which they can, according to Toury, reconstruct the norms themselves. The reconstructed norm could be called the "practical norm," whereas the direct normative pronouncements or pre-systematic formulations of norms could be termed "theoretical norms." Toury warns his reader to treat the latter with the utmost circumspection, since they are not only partial and accidental but also likely to be biased. Analysts should compare as many of these pre-systematic formulations to each other as possible, and hold them up against the norms reconstructed from the texts themselves. Such a process of comparison would, of course, serve to verify, refute or correct *both* sets of norms.[24] Unfortunately, Toury offers the reader few guidelines concerning the crucial moment in the descriptive analysis: the reconstruction of translational norms from translated texts themselves. With regard to matricial norms he does, however, refer to notions used in traditional rhetoric, such as omission, addition, permutation, and substitution.

The notion of translational norms can be further developed as a category for the analysis of translation phenomena. Descriptive translation studies need not be limited to the comparison of one source text to one translated text. Important conclusions about the change of norms can be drawn from the comparison of one source text with several translated texts. The corpus can be enlarged still further if we examine not only the different translations of one source text within one particular literature, but different translations of a particular original within different literatures and cultures. An investigation of a series of translations of the same original within different literary systems and cultures allows one to arrive at conclusions with respect to the relative position translated literature occupies and the function it assumes within and among these different cultures. Translations, evidently, play an active role in the contact and communication between different cultures. Each culture receives a foreign text differently. Hence, Toury's translational norms are an important tool for a descriptive model, which views translation as a form of cultural intercommunication and negotiation, since these translational norms reveal the national prejudices and cultural characteristics which underscore translation practice.

Translational norms can be derived from extratextual information (statements by translators, publishers, editors, critics) which projects a "horizon of expectation" for the translation under investigation. But they are primarily revealed by the comparative examination of source and translated text. Here Toury has unnecessarily complicated his method of analysis by introducing a theory-dependent invariant or *tertium comparationis* which the researcher has to establish before attempting to relate the translated text to the original. The target text will thus be compared with a hypothetical third text, an "adequate" translation formulated in the target language but still source-text-oriented in that only "obligatory shifts" are taken into account. (Obligatory shifts are "rule-governed" changes which cannot be avoided in translation, such as the substitution of French *vous* when marked for politeness in French by the unmarked "you" in English.) The comparison of the target text with this intermediary constant should then automatically reveal the more interesting optional shifts (caused by factors other than grammatical rules) and thus the prevailing translational norms. According to Toury this intermediary construction of the adequate translation (the *tertium comparationis*) should ideally be formulated in a formal language, but such a language is not available. Another problem with his notion is that it presupposes a clear-cut distinction between obligatory and optional shifts. It is not always so clear which syntactical shifts, for instance, are optional and which are obligatory. The answer to this question ultimately depends on the assumed tolerance of the target reader; it may differ from culture to culture, from period to period, and from genre to genre and it is therefore subject to translational norms as well as to the conditions governing the target polysystem. A *tertium comparationis* not only complicates the comparative study of a translation with the original text serving as its source, it may also distort its actual findings.[25] No reading, analysis, translation or comparison can hope to be disinterested. Just as the translator will derive "maps" of the source text during the formulation of the translated text, the analyst will use a mental conception of both the source text and the translated text in his or her description of the relationships between these texts. Toury proposes to derive this *tertium comparationis* from a thorough analysis of the source text. Such an analysis is by itself, without any additional intermediate construction, indeed the most obvious guide for comparing original and translated texts.[26]

Whereas Even-Zohar's and Toury's studies primarily focus on the description of translations (as products) and their position in the target literature, James S Holmes investigates the translation process itself. In an essay entitled "Describing Literary Translations: Models and Methods" (1978), Holmes argues that before one can develop relevant methods for the description of translation products, it is first of all necessary to develop an adequate model of the translation process.[27] In other words, while Even-Zohar and Toury attempt to draw a distinction between product- and process-oriented studies, Holmes maintains that they cannot be separated. After having presented a description of the translation process as a "two-map two-plane text-rank translation model," he goes on to consider the task of the analyst who hopes to describe the relationship between translation and original.[28]

In his description of that relationship, Holmes focuses on the reconstruction of the translator's two maps and the "correspondence rules" determining their relationship. In his model, the descriptive analyst derives a list of distinctive features from the two texts (original and translation) and determines a hierarchical ordering of their features. This method, according to Holmes, "remains to a large extent an *ad hoc* operation."[29] The maps (or "mental conception") of the two texts (original and translation) reconstructed by the analyst, like the translator's two maps derived from the source text, will always remain incomplete. In other words, Holmes recognizes the hermeneutic aspect of both the translation process and the process of describing or analyzing translations. Translation and its description or analysis are socio-historical activities guided by personal or larger cultural concerns. What constitutes a map for one interpreter obviously does not constitute a map for another interpreter. Their maps are not so much incomplete but rather the products of different structuration processes which are largely determined by different socio-cultural codes. Robert de Beaugrande even suggests in his *Factors in a Theory of Poetic Translating* that we need to take into account questions such as the translator's "socio-economic status, education and training, knowledge and beliefs drawn from experience, personal interests and priorities, and the constellation surrounding the act of using language," since these are factors that determine the translator's decision-making process.[30]

The definition of translating as a series of decisions and choices rather than as a process of blindly following mechanical rules is also proposed by Jiří Levý in his essay on "Translation as a Decision Process."[31] He characterizes translation from a teleological point of view as a "PROCESS OF COMMUNICATION," and translating from the pragmatic point of view ("from the point of view of the working situation of the translator at any moment of his work") as a "DECISION PROCESS: a series of a certain number of consecutive situations – moves as in a game – situations imposing on the translator the necessity of choosing among a certain (and very often exactly definable) number of alternatives."[32] Levý recognizes that translation involves both interpretation and creation, and stresses the fact that "every interpretation has the structure of problem solving."[33] Obviously, the choices translators make are not random but context-bound, and once they have decided in favor of one of the alternatives, they have to a large extent predetermined their own choices in a number of subsequent moves. That is to say, "the process of translating has the form of a GAME WITH COMPLETE INFORMATION – a game in which every succeeding move is influenced by the knowledge of previous decisions and by the situation which resulted from them (e.g. chess, but not card-games)."[34] One possible approach to translation theory, according to Levý, is

> to take into account all the subsequent decisions contingent on the given choice, and hence to trace the order of precedence for the solving of the different problems and the resulting degree of importance of various elements in the literary work, when considered from this viewpoint.[35]

The outcome of two series of decisions, for instance, resulting from two alternative interpretations, would, according to Levý, quite simply be what he terms two different translation variants, whose difference, or distance from each other, can be measured by comparing the separate translation decisions incorporated into each text. Levý thus emphasizes that, whereas translation theory tends to be normative, in that it stresses idealized, "optimal" solutions to translation problems, actual translation work is pragmatic, inasmuch as translators usually weigh solutions according to their propensity to supply maximum effect for a minimum of effort on their part and on that of readers in the receiving culture.[36]

Levý reveals the profoundly transformative nature of translation when he represents it first and foremost as a decision-making process, according to which a translator's decisions are not exclusively based on his or her interpretation of the original text but are also made with a certain goal in mind. Translation is seen as both an interpretative and a teleological activity. Unfortunately, Levý offers us few insights (beyond the purely linguistic and stylistic level) into the motivations underlying the translator's decisions. However, in dismissing the notion of translation as a rule-governed activity and substituting for it the notion of an active decision-making process, Levý points to the "shifts" which inevitably occur in a translation.

Translation as a (communication and) decision-making process necessarily entails shifts, and as such Levý does not consider their presence as evidence of a defeatist strategy or a last resort on the part of the translator. On the contrary, they are the inevitable result of an encounter between two series of linguistic, intertextual and cultural norms or codes. The basic problem facing translators, according to Holmes, is that they must not only "shift" the original to another linguistic context, but also to a different literary intertext and to a different sociocultural situation.[37] In his essay entitled "Rebuilding the Bridge at Bommel," Holmes argues that translational problems can be situated at each of these three levels and that a translation results in a "shift" at each of them.[38] He represents the translator's choice pattern during the translation process as being drawn from two axes: "exoticizing versus naturalizing" and "historicizing versus modernizing." Choices made along the "exoticizing versus naturalizing" axis concern the translator's decision either to retain a specific element of the original linguistic context, the literary intertext, or the sociocultural situation, "knowing that in the new context, intertext, and situation, that element will acquire an exotic aspect not attached to it in its native habitat," or to replace that element with one that he or she considers will in some way "match" the target context, intertext, or situation.[39] Choices made along the "historicizing versus modernizing" axis reflect another series of decisions. Either translators try to evoke both the historical flavor of the setting and the time-bound language usage of the original in the translated text by selecting comparable historical solutions on the linguistic, literary, and socio-historical levels, or they render the original more up to date in terms of the period in which they work. The two axes basically indicate choices of time and space involved in the translation process. With the introduction of these two polar alternatives Holmes also reacts against some theorists' conviction that "choices should be all of a piece: all exoticizing and historicizing, with an emphasis on *retention*, or all naturalizing and modernizing, with an emphasis on *re-creation*."[40] In Holmes' opinion, it is virtually impossible to make all one's translation choices along one axis: in practice, translators find themselves having to make a series of pragmatic choices, "here retentive, there re-creative, at that point modernizing or naturalizing, and emphasizing now this plane now that, at the cost of the other two."[41]

Corroborating Levý's conception of translation as a largely transformative, teleological activity, Lawrence Venuti further emphasizes that translation is a social activity governed by cultural norms. In his essay on "The Translator's Invisibility," he describes the translator's situation and praxis in contemporary Anglo-American culture.[42] By the term "invisibility" Venuti is referring to the reader's response to translations, as well as to the criteria by which translations are produced and evaluated. Readers often respond to translations as "naturalized" or "nationalized" works which are virtually indistinguishable from the original works they read in their own language and culture. Translations in Anglo-American culture are indeed judged acceptable and publishable when they read fluently, when there is no hint of any linguistic or cultural interferences from the source culture. Venuti perceives the translator's invisibility on two fronts: textual or aesthetic, and especially socio-economic. Although social determinants are external to the translated text, they are nevertheless inscribed in its materiality. Venuti relates the contemporary call for fluency or easy readability to bourgeois economic values: consumability and individualism. Both ideologies, in his opinion, determine that the original text "will be translated and read in a way that can reproduce the capitalist relations of production in which it is situated."[43]

It is possible to criticize Venuti by pointing out that his notion of bourgeois consumability, which he finds characteristic of the capitalist mode of production, could also be applied to its polar opposite, communist translation ideology, which likewise favors the strategy of fluency and easy readability. In both cases, this strategy allows for the reproduction of the given social conditions and relations of production. Venuti's article makes it quite clear, however, that translation is first and foremost a socio-cultural activity: the choice of foreign texts to be translated, the interpretative decisions opted for during the translation process, the dissemination, reception, and evaluation of the translated texts themselves are all considerably determined by the socio-cultural context in which they function.

Whereas Venuti largely discusses translation as a code abiding type of exercise or as a strategy of conformity to contemporary Anglo-American culture (and, by extension, the culture of the capitalist world at large), Barbara Harlow views translation as "a strategy of cultural resistance," or a code-changing activity when she addresses translation problems that occur in so-called "Third World" countries. Her paper entitled "From Deconstruction to Decolonization: The Political Agenda of Translation" depicts translation as "a political strategy of communication between divided communities," that can either be promoted or discouraged by the authorities in the receiving culture.[44] Harlow examines several cases of translation and censorship in those areas of the world where the influence of Western metaphysics is wielded largely through the politics of colonialism and imperialism, in particular in North Africa and the Middle East. Here she sees translation as a "strategy of cultural resistance." Harlow interprets several historical situations and texts which support her argument. Colonialism on the part of French settlers in Algeria, for instance, suppressed indigenous Arabic literary production. Consequently, when Algeria achieved independence, a critical part of its national agenda was a process of "Arabization" in all spheres of public and institutional activity. Yet, many North African writers and intellectuals have continued to produce their work in French. The francophony of North African writers, Harlow remarks, entails a certain calculated irony: it allows them to distance themselves from the French language by inverting it, destroying it, and presenting new structures to the point where French readers would feel like strangers in their own language.[45]

As both Venuti and Harlow demonstrate, each interpreter and/or translator performs, in Fredric Jameson's words, "something like an allegorical operation in which a text is systematically *rewritten* in terms of some fundamental master code, or 'ultimately determining instance'."[46] The master code determining the translations produced in contemporary Anglo-American culture is variously defined by Venuti as "invisibility," "fluency," "consumability," and, in general, as the reproduction of the capitalist relations of production. The master code that makes translations acceptable in, for instance, North Africa and Lebanon, is pinpointed by Harlow as "Arabization." In his paper "Translation Studies and/in Comparative Literature," André Lefevere argues that if texts are not translated, i.e. "rewritten" in terms of a "master code," if they cannot be integrated into the "master code" that is dominant in a given society at a given time, they quite simply do not exist. He infers that if

> all writing about literature is, essentially, rewriting the work of literature in the service of some master code, then all writing on literature becomes, essentially, manipulation: the original is made to fit somewhere in the territory mapped out by a certain master code.[47]

Jameson's suggestion for critical practice in light of these master codes is "to acquire the instruments by which we can force a given interpretive practice to stand and yield up its name, to blurt out its master code and thereby reveal its metaphysical and ideological underpinnings."[48] Lefevere picks up on this idea and reasons that if all writing on literature is rewriting or a manipulation of literature in the service of a master code, then "the study of literature becomes the study of the ways in which that manipulation takes place."[49] This manipulation is most transparent and can be shown most readily at work in the case of translation. Hence, Lefevere argues for a framework of literary studies in which interpretation itself becomes the problem. In such a framework translation occupies a central position, because it serves as the locus where the manipulation can be shown most clearly and also most simply – by working with facing texts, one the original, the other the translation. Not unlike Harlow, Lefevere makes it clear that analysts of translation must deal with issues that are not limited to the question of how a text is translated: they must also be aware of the reasons why a text was selected for translation in the first instance, the identity of the translator, and his or her success or failure in meeting a set of translational aims.[50] In other words, translation has to do with much more than language; it is also a question of power.

Jameson's notion of the "master code" and Lefevere's reading of this notion highlight the motivations, norms, and values underlying any socio-cultural praxis, including translation. Yet the notion of a "master code" may not be entirely free of interpretation itself: it may even be a question of "blindness and insight" on Jameson's part, in that by focusing on one particular master code he may fail to determine the presence of another, equally "masterful" allegory. The least one can say is that this notion needs to be historicized and perhaps even modified, since it appears to be yet another transcendental instance in itself. A particular "master code" need not completely determine or "overpower" a certain praxis. Not all texts can be wholly reduced to one specific master code which governs them or is read into them. However, given these reservations, it is nonetheless possible to see literary works or literary translations as not only conforming to, but also as standing in a dialogic relationship with, one or more metaphysically rooted master codes.

The aim of this introduction has been to move toward a model of translation which is historical-relative and socio-cultural. It seeks to depict translation as a process of negotiation between two (or more) series of cultural codes and systems, as the product of "transcoding" different cultures, and not solely as the result of a crossing of linguistic barriers. Translation should not be considered a matter of equivalence or synonymy, but rather one of differences and shifts, since it entails a goal-oriented decision-making process of negotiation between various cultural codes and systems.

Even-Zohar's hypotheses with regard to translated literature contain several useful notions for the development of a model for the study of translation, notably the idea that the literary polysystem forms part of the larger polysystem of a culture. The intricate correlations within this larger cultural system (society, economy, ideology, literature, language, etc.) are seen as isomorphic in nature. They are functional only within a cultural whole, and can be observed on the basis of the mutual give-and-take which often occurs obliquely between them through transformational devices. Consequently, translated literature, which functions largely on the periphery of the polysystem, operates as a cultural, semiotic system which interacts with all other semiotic co-systems.

Translation is not, as some would have it, a derivative or secondary literary activity. As a form of interliterary communication it is a unique sign-producing act whereby the translator must choose between different sets of cultural norms and values. Literary translation can, in fact, be seen as a creatively controlled process of acculturation, in that translators can take an original text and adapt it to a certain dominant poetics or ideology in the receiving culture. They can also devise some kind of compromise between two different sets of poetics or ideologies, one belonging to the source culture and the other to the target culture. Furthermore, a translator can import a foreign text with little attempt to acculturate its unfamiliar form for the receiving culture. Out of dissatisfaction (for ideological or other reasons) with the dominant poetics or ideology of the receiving literature, translators can turn to a foreign text in order to introduce a new poetic model which may serve as an attack on canonical forms in that literature. Since translations have to negotiate between at least two distinct cultural codes and systems, they can be shaped by the translator to join one side of the battle for primacy between different literary or ideological schools of thought by disrupting or interrupting the master codes of the receiving culture. Attention to historical and cultural constraints operating in the receiving culture will make practising translators more aware of the reasons for their decisions when they translate, and at the same time lead them away from the very normative approaches to translation that have limited their activities in the past.

The historical function of translated literature is, perhaps, most apparent in the creation of new poetic models. Translations enable the transfer of literary devices and models from one literature or culture to another and thus enrich developing literatures in need of poetic models or renew established literatures that find themselves in crisis. Furthermore, translated literature occupies a unique position, given its ability to function as an intermediary between at least two literatures, and thus two cultures: it has the potential to demonstrate characteristics of the source literature as well as of the receiving literature. The study of translations may thus add significantly to knowledge of the interaction between literary systems and may tell both readers and theorists something about the ways in which these systems function. It should not be overlooked, however, that it is the "target" literature which initiates the "literary contact," and that this receiving literary system can either accept or reject the translated original. What is translated and how certain works or items come to be translated is determined in relation to the interests and the organization of the receiving literary system. Literary works or devices are not mechanically transplanted from one particular source literature to a receiving literature but transformed by the translator to accommodate or disrupt models operative in the receiving culture. Thus the receiving literature filters out some of the original's components, and necessarily changes the role the original played in the source literature. If a translation is to function successfully in the receiving literature, the translator must do more than switch language codes. In fact, linguistic barriers seem almost trivial if one takes into account the different historical and socio-cultural backgrounds as well as the different literary codes operating in the receiving literature. Furthermore, if translators seek the acceptance of their translation of a literary text as "literature," they will have to face what Hans Robert Jauss calls the "horizon of expectation" (*Erwartungshorizont*) of the receiving literature.[51] Some clue as to the success or failure of a translation when subjected to this most acid of tests is provided, on the most obvious level, by examining the critical responses it elicited in reviews. Furthermore, the general horizon of expectation of a literature at a particular time can be gauged by referring to critical, historiographical and encyclopedic works covering literary debate contemporary to the translation. Such works, by their very nature, indicate what was considered to constitute "literature" at a certain period in time, and in addition reveal which works and writers approximated that ideal and which ones did not.

Once in the hands of readers in the target culture, some translations may be regarded as "bizarre" or "exotic" and may be rejected by a majority of those who come into contact with them; others, too neutral or flat, are hardly noticed as "translations" and merge with the original works of the receiving literature; still others that negotiate and introduce a compromise may attain a canonized position in that literature. In terms of the receiving literary system, the adopted translational norms may appear at first to be too foreign and revolutionary, and if the new trend is defeated in a literary power struggle the translations made according to these norms stand little chance of ever gaining ground. But if the new trend is victorious, the code of translated literature is enriched and becomes more flexible. When translational activity participates in the process of creating new models, it assumes a "primary" position in the literary polysystem of the receiving culture. As noted by Even-Zohar, from the point of view of translational behavior such periods are almost the only ones when translators are prepared to go far beyond the options offered to them by the established codes in the receiving culture. However, under stable conditions, specific translational items such as genres or poetic devices lacking in a receiving literature may remain untransferred if the state of the cultural polysystem does not allow for innovations.

If it is accepted that translation is, above all, a form of cultural negotiation, then it is possible at last to propose a historical-relative, socio-cultural model that allows for the identification of at least three kinds of translation: (1) translations that do not really attempt to acculturate the original work; the translator adheres to the cultural codes that inform the source culture: the translated original is perceived as "exotic" and "bizarre" and will most likely stay on the periphery of the receiving culture; (2) translations that negotiate and introduce a cultural compromise; these translations confront the problem of communication by selecting and balancing characteristics common to both source and receiving culture: the translator has altered the codes of the receiving culture in such a way that those confronted with the alteration will at the same time recognize the alteration and the code; the translated original may attain a canonized position in the receiving culture; and (3) translations that completely acculturate the original work;

the translator adheres to the codes which inform the receiving culture: the translated original may attain a canonized position or stay on the periphery of the receiving culture. Translations that completely acculturate the original work could be expected to "modernize" and "naturalize" the three textual dimensions of linguistic context, literary intertext, and sociocultural situation. Such translations would also tend to exploit the strategy of "fluency" or "easy readability" where the role of the translator becomes invisible or transparent. The strategy of cultural resistance as a code-changing activity relates to the first or second type of translation in which the translator seeks to retain as much of the foreign source culture as possible, even at the risk of being misunderstood by the receiving culture.

This model does not seek to satisfy all questions of rigorous classification; rather it presents itself as a broad review of the possibilities open to the translator in which translations range from the "exotic" (case one) to the "familiar" (case three). These case-types have not been presented in order of their likely application to one foreign original: indeed they do not all have to be present in a particular culture in order to admit a foreign original. The model serves as a working hypothesis which attempts to explain translation in terms of "acculturation." In addition, over time, the three types of translation may shift their position within the receiving culture: for instance, translations which hardly transform the cultural codes pertaining to the original may take up a primary position within the receiving literature under certain conditions. This model needs to be historicized when examining existing translations so that it does not impose the very rigorous classification it tries to avoid.[52]

As can be inferred from the above, translation should not be seen as a rule-regulated activity but a decision-making process. The decisions a translator has to make in interpreting and transcoding a foreign text inevitably make translation a teleological activity, whereby the translator actively intervenes and appropriates the foreign text with a particular objective in mind. Translation is thereby revealed as a socio-historical activity of a profoundly transformative nature. It is not really a question of identity or synonymy but rather one of differences and shifts. All translations are goal- and audience-oriented, since they are not produced in a cultural vacuum. Normative theories can only evaluate translations in terms of "good" and "bad." A model that calls attention to the socio-historical conditions informing the translator's activity offers a clearer insight into the mechanisms that allow translations to function in the receiving culture. By underlining the translator's active intervention in appropriating and acculturating a foreign text, the underlying motives and the decisions which inform the translational process, it is possible to reach a better understanding of the process by which existing translations are created.

Chapter 1

Jean-François Ducis' *Hamlet, Tragédie imitée de l'anglois*
A neoclassical tragedy?

Shakespeare was largely an unknown quantity in France until the early eighteenth century, when a combination of factors resulted in his becoming the most popular foreign playwright in the country. The first translations of episodes from Shakespeare, by Destouches and the Abbé Leblanc, contributed to a wave of anglomania, which was in turn further fueled by the *Lettres philosophiques*, in which Voltaire translated selected passages of Shakespeare into French, and even went so far as to compare the Englishman to Homer ("Essai sur la poésie épique").

In 1745, Antoine de La Place published *Le Théâtre anglois*, containing translations of *Hamlet* and nine other Shakespearian plays.[1] These were by no means complete versions of the original plays: La Place had translated only what he considered the most striking passages and linked them together by means of plot synopses. Nevertheless, La Place's efforts still further popularized Shakespeare among the intelligentsia: his translations were not meant to be acted, but to stimulate salon conversation by providing the French literati with a glimpse of something far removed from the conventions of their own classical theatre. By presenting his work as closet drama (that is, not intended to be staged), La Place was able to depict ghosts, swordfighting, murder, and all manner of plot lines Racine would never have dared to show on stage.

Presenting his Shakespeare as closet drama did not, however, afford La Place the luxury of translating Shakespeare's blank verse. The following passage, composed in beautifully flowing alexandrines, could have been taken from Racine, had it not been delivered by a ghost, but is in fact from La Place's *Hamlet* (I, v, 9–17):

LE SPECTRE. Tu vois ton Père!...Un arrêt rigoureux,
　　　　　　 Mais juste, le condamne à des tourmens affreux,
　　　　　　 Jusqu'à l'heureux instant où l'Eternel propice
　　　　　　 Fera cesser des maux qu'exige sa justice.
　　　　　　 Que ne puis-je tracer cet effrayant tableau,
　　　　　　 Que l'oeil mortel ne voit, qu'en entrant au
　　　　　　　　 tombeau?
　　　　　　 Tu frémirois, mon fils, à l'aspect de mes peines,
　　　　　　 Et je verrois ton sang se figer dans tes veines,
　　　　　　 Je verrois sur ton front l'épouvante et la mort.[2]

[You see your father before you....
A harsh but just confinement to wander the
　　earth
Has condemned him to suffer horrible
　　torments
Until the joyous moment when the Eternal one
Will cause these ills his justice has demanded to
　　cease.
How can I describe this horrible scene,
The mortal eye sees only on entering the tomb?
You would tremble, my son, at the sight of my
　　pains,
And I would see your blood coagulate in your
　　veins,
I would see in your face both terror and death.]

La Place's translations became the talk of the salons: very soon their popularity and that of Shakespeare threatened to dethrone even Corneille and Racine. Voltaire, who had previously been so enthusiastic, now began to fear that the dissemination of such foreign material would contaminate the neoclassical ideals of French theatre. As late as 1770, he had referred to Shakespeare as "a genius" ("Du théâtre anglais"). However, once it became clear that Shakespeare's works constituted a threat to the old order, with the appearance of more comprehensive, less fragmentary translations of the plays by Jean-François Ducis (1770) and Pierre Le Tourneur (1776), Voltaire spoke out:

> What is frightful is that this monster has support in France; and, at the height of calamity and horror, it was I who in the past first spoke of this Shakespeare; it was I who was the first

to point out to Frenchmen the few pearls which were to be found in this enormous dunghill. It never entered my mind that by doing so I would one day assist the effort to trample on the crowns of Racine and Corneille in order to wreathe the brow of this barbaric mountebank.[3]

The above letter was written in 1776, more than thirty years after the appearance of La Place's first closet translations of Shakespeare. The deciding factor in securing Voltaire's opposition to an English tragic model seems to have been the stupendous success enjoyed by the first stage production of Ducis' translation of *Hamlet*, which received its premiere in 1769. Ducis, as it happens, did not fit the traditional image of a translator, in that he spoke no English. "Je n'entends point l'Anglois," he stated in the "Avertissement" to his version of *Hamlet*, "et j'ai osé faire paroître Hamlet sur la Scene Françoise." [I don't understand a word of English and yet I have presumed to put Hamlet on the French stage.] [4] His translation of the play was initially based on La Place's synopsis, to which Voltaire had not objected; later versions included some textual changes drawn from Le Tourneur's 1776 prose *Hamlet*.

What seems to have bothered Voltaire, however, is the idea of the success of a "barbaric" foreign play at the Comédie Française, the very cradle of the neoclassical ideal. Although Ducis' translation at first sight seems to have been composed according to a neoclassical stage model, on further examination it reveals itself to be something else entirely. It seems likely that Voltaire saw in Ducis' translation, and in the very success it enjoyed, the seeds of the imminent destruction of classical tragedy as he knew it.

Ducis, as a translator, took La Place's bare synopsis as an intermediary translation on which to base his version (or as he calls it his "imitation") of *Hamlet*. He then altered and rearranged the plot, cut down the list of players, and composed an unbroken, playable text, written in alexandrines, with all the appearance of a classic tragedy. What was not so evident was Ducis' use of his translation of *Hamlet* to introduce a new theatrical model, bourgeois drama, to the repertory of the Comédie Française, by cloaking it in neoclassical garb.

Paradoxically, Ducis' *Hamlet* did more for Shakespeare than it did for bourgeois drama. Not only was it the catalyst for all subsequent French translations of Shakespeare, but it was the basis for the first Italian (1772), Spanish (1772), Dutch (1777), Swedish, and Russian translations of the play.[5] It stayed in the repertory of the Comédie Française until 1851, outlasting not only the "sentimental comedies" of Marivaux, but the whole tenure of Romanticism.

As a translator, Ducis never claimed to have reproduced Shakespeare as an English audience would have recognized him. Indeed he even wrote a letter to Garrick, apologizing for the changes he had imposed on the piece:

> I imagine, sir, that you must have found me extremely rash to put a play such as *Hamlet* onto the French stage. Without even mentioning the wild irregularities which abound throughout, the ghost, which I admit plays a large part, the rustic actors and the swordplay, seemed to me to be devices which are absolutely inadmissible on our stage. However, I deeply regretted not being able to introduce the public to the fearsome spectre that exposes the crime and demands vengeance. So I was forced, in a way, to create a new play. I just tried to make an interesting character of the parricidal queen and above all to depict the pure and melancholic Hamlet as a model of filial tenderness.[6]

From this letter one can infer that Ducis' "initial norm" or the basic choice he made as a translator was to subject himself completely to the conventions operative in the French theatre, those expected of a playwright by both institution and audience. When he claims to have created "a new play" from Shakespeare's original, it is apparent that this play has been made to resemble other contemporary French tragedies. Due to the Académie Française's veto on matters of taste, Ducis was effectively forced to change the matrix or the textual material of the original, otherwise he would have had no hope of ever presenting the play at the Comédie Française. His selection of suitable French "tragic" material to replace some of the original scenes, in other words the textual and matricial norms to which Ducis adhered, were determined by the typical French neoclassical play and, less evidently, by eighteenth-century bourgeois drama. In order to assure the play's acceptance by the Comédie Française, Ducis made the following changes to Shakespeare's dramatic text. Gone are the actor playing the

Ghost, the traveling players (and consequently the play within the play), the combat scene at the end between Hamlet and Laertes and no fewer than fifteen of the original twenty-three characters! Ducis knew that his *Hamlet* would stand more of a chance of impressing the readers at the Comédie Française if he was able to uncover those "few pearls" of which Voltaire talked, and to make them fit the classical triad of *bienséance*, *ordre*, and *vraisemblance*, or verisimilitude. His approach (on the surface, one of complete acculturation) was at the time the only way of making Shakespeare available to the French theatregoing public. Without the modifications he made, it is open to question when if ever Shakespeare would have been performed at the Comédie Française.

Ducis' translation brings forth the genius of *Hamlet*, but subject to the classical canon. He "naturalized" Shakespeare's *Hamlet* for an audience used to the structures of neoclassicism. It appears to be an idealized and acculturated *Hamlet*, showing what Shakespeare would have written had he been a contemporary and a compatriot of Racine, a case of the French appreciating foreign genius but at the same time saying to themselves, "Ah yes, if only he had been French," as opposed to Le Tourneur's more source text oriented prose translation, which brought out Shakespeare "the barbarian," and was presumably perceived at the time as "exotic" or "bizarre" due to its failure to acculturate the English material.

In order to conform to the French tragic blueprint, Ducis departed not only from Shakespeare but also from La Place's matricial norms. There is a different plot, the relationships between the main characters have been altered, and the unities of time, place, and action are observed. All the action takes place in Elsinore, within the required twenty-four-hour period, with all the characters passing through an antechamber in the castle to deliver their speeches. Unity of action means that all the sub-plots of the original, the play within the play, the death of Ophelia, the gravediggers' scene, and Hamlet's "Alas poor Yorick" meditation have been discarded. As Peter Conroy points out, the character of "Ophélie" represents, to the French classical audience, an unnecessary diversion in much the same way as the character of the Infante did in *Le Cid*, drawing the audience's attention away from the main plot.[7] Voltaire wrote that, despite his initial enthusiasm for *Hamlet*, he had not been able to overcome his sense of shock at seeing comic interludes in a tragedy, and therefore could not focus on Hamlet's meditations on death. Ducis correspondingly dropped any scenes which involved the slightest notion of comedy, such as the one with the gravediggers, to avoid incongruity of tone. Needless to say, his translation entailed a generic shift from tragi-comedy to what appeared on the surface to be pure neoclassical tragedy.[8]

In order to recreate the *personnel habituel* of classical tragedy, Ducis was forced to prune the list of players. Hamlet becomes king of Denmark, though as yet uncrowned. Claudius is next in line to the throne, but he is no longer the brother of the late king. Gertrude, who remains the late king's widow, now has a confidante, Elvire, whose principal dramatic function is to be a foil for her mistress, and to allow the action to develop through dialogue. Ophelia is now the daughter, not of Polonius, but of Claudius. Polonius is the confidant and agent of Claudius. Horatio has been replaced by a character called Norceste, Hamlet's childhood friend and confidant. Voltimand is a confidant with no master, having a walk-on part as the captain of the guard to fill the gaps created by the absence of Rosencrantz, Guildenstern, and, most surprising of all perhaps, Laertes. The list of characters is rounded off by some unnamed guards.

As for the background to the play, Claudius is at first presented as a nobleman who has been wronged by the late king. It later emerges he was the perpetrator of the regicide: Gertrude had plotted with him but she had repented at the last minute and tried to warn the king of the danger. She had planned to marry Claudius, but now regrets her part in the affair and is doing all she can to assure the coronation of her son instead. Hamlet is in love with Ophelia, the daughter of the man he hates, his rival for the throne. Polonius is presented as Claudius' co-conspirator, who listens to the latter's plans to ascend to the throne by marrying Gertrude or by overthrowing Hamlet.

Hamlet retains his trademark of dark depression, caused by the Ghost's appearance to him in his dreams. The Ghost urges the still uncrowned king to avenge his death by killing Gertrude and Claudius. Norceste listens to Hamlet's story of murder and advises him to test Gertrude's guilt or innocence before resolving to kill her. Hamlet also confides in Ophelia about the Ghost and proceeds to prove his mother's guilt in a famous scene made wildly popular by the actor Talma, in which he confronts Gertrude with the urn containing the king's ashes which had been given to him by Norceste for that purpose. Her guilt is proven when she faints at Hamlet's challenge to deny her part in the plot before the altar represented by the urn. Yet Hamlet finds himself unable to kill his own mother and resolves to satisfy his father's demands by slaying Claudius. The pretender, meanwhile, is plotting against Hamlet when his daughter, Ophelia, tries to change his mind. Hamlet and Claudius finally come face to face, and Claudius reveals that he has killed Gertrude himself, for standing in the way of his plot to overthrow Hamlet. Before Claudius can call in his fellow conspirators to kill Hamlet, the latter stabs him (out of the sight of the audience), thereby avenging his father.

Such was the plot of Ducis' first edition of *Hamlet*, published in 1770.[9] As will be noted, only an echo of Shakespeare's original dramatic material is retained. Hamlet still hesitates before his task, but the opportunity to avenge the death of both his parents by killing Claudius finally spurs him into action. The play conforms to the classical requirements of *bienséance* by eliminating the duel between Hamlet and Laertes, as well as Gertrude's drinking of the poisoned wine. Claudius' death is actually obscured behind the crowd of conspirators who rush forward to kill Hamlet on the occasion of his coronation, but the limits of *bienséance* were still stretched by the fact that Claudius' death actually occurred on the stage. However, in subsequent versions of the play, this ending was replaced by the expedient of both Claudius and Gertrude committing suicide or, in another variant, by Hamlet killing Claudius in the wings. In the 1770 version the Ghost does not of course appear on stage, except in Hamlet's mind. Hamlet addresses his famous "To be or not to be" monologue to the same funeral urn containing the dead king's ashes with which he later confronts the queen. The presence of the urn satisfies the requirements of decorum in a way the Ghost would be unable to do, while still preserving an allusion to the original plot.

The classical virtues of balance and symmetry are also present in Ducis' text. Gertrude is torn between loyalty to her son and her lover, Hamlet between his love for Ophelia and his hatred of Claudius. Then there is the whole set of parallel master–confidant relationships: Claudius–Polonius; Gertrude–Elvire; Hamlet–Norceste; and the chiastic pattern: (active) Claudius–Ophelia (passive); (passive) Gertrude–Hamlet (active). This set of relationships mirrors the symmetry of the plot (all five acts open with master–confidant scenes, even Act IV, which begins with Hamlet confiding in Norceste, and then in the urn). The first two acts, in traditional classical style, are devoted to the exposition and the preparation of the events to come. Acts III and IV build up the suspense, and the culmination of the tragedy occurs in Act V. Action has been reduced to a bare minimum, and the real focus of the play is on the brilliantly executed alexandrines which make up the *récits*, or classical monologues. These *récits* assume real importance since they describe action which now takes place offstage – the classical filtering of action through language which establishes the play as a verbal entity, revolving around carefully chosen vocabulary.

In contrast to Le Tourneur, who courted scandal by attempting to reproduce Shakespeare's verbal imagery in his closet prose translation of *Hamlet*, Ducis preferred to produce a *Hamlet* which had been exposed to the French classical tradition of Racine and Voltaire.[10] Not only did this mean that Shakespeare's vocabulary was reduced to a restricted number of words heavy with tragic connotations, invested with the power and significance of the French tragic canon, but also that Shakespeare's duality and punning were totally eliminated, along with any words deemed common or vulgar in tone. To illustrate Ducis' use of language and the plot alterations he made, the following is the whole of Hamlet's soliloquy from IV, iii of Ducis' 1770 version (roughly equivalent to III, i in Shakespeare):

Ah! je respire enfin, je n'ai donc plus d'amour.
Je puis à ma fureur me livrer sans retour.
    [*En regardant l'urne*
Gage de mes sermens, urne terrible & sainte
Que j'invoque en pleurant, que j'embrasse avec crainte,
C'est à vous d'affermir mon bras prêt à frapper.
Barbare Claudius, ne crois pas m'échapper.
Mais quand j'aurai cent fois ma vengeance assouvie,
Est-il en mon pouvoir de te rendre la vie,

Mon trop malheureux père? Ah! Prince infortuné,
Ou pourquoi n'es-tu plus, ou pourquoi suis-je né?
Eh, quoi! ton noble aspect, ton auguste visage,
Au moment du forfait n'ont point fléchi leur rage?
Les cruels ... ils ont pu ... tu ne jouiras pas,
Perfide empoisonneur, du fruit de son trépas.
Je crois déjà, je crois, dans ma vengeance avide,
Presser ton coeur sanglant dans ton sein parricide.
Oui, perfide, oui, cruel; ces mains vont t'immoler;
Voici l'autel terrible où ton sang va couler.
Mais de mon père, ô ciel! je sens frémir la cendre.
Mes transports jusqu'à lui se sont-ils fait entendre?
O poudre des tombeaux, qui vous vient agiter?
Est-ce pour m'affermir, ou pour m'épouvanter?
Cendre plaintive & chère, oui, j'entends ton murmure:
Oui, ce poignard sanglant va laver ton injure;
C'étoit pour te venger que j'ai souffert le jour.
C'en est fait, je te venge, & je meurs à mon tour.
Mais que vois-je?

[Ah, I can finally breathe, my love is no longer here.
I can give myself up to my fury forever.
      [*looks at urn*
Dread and holy urn, I tearfully invoke you
I embrace you with fear, I pledge by my oath, you must strengthen my arm to strike.
Barbarous Claudius, do not think you have escaped me.
But when I have satisfied my vengeance one hundredfold
Is it in my power to restore you to life,
My unfortunate father? Ah! wretched prince,
Why do you no longer live? Why was I born?
What? Your noble bearing, your majestic features
Did they not soften the murderers' rage at the moment of truth?
The blackguards ... they were able ...
You will not reap, treacherous poisoner,
The fruit of his demise.
I can see myself now, in my thirst for vengeance
Squeezing your bloody heart within your parricidal breast
Yes, cruel traitor, these hands will slay you
Here on the terrible altar upon which your blood will flow.

What of my father, o heaven! I feel the ashes tremble.
Have my raptures made their way to his ears?
O, dust from the tomb, what has shaken you?
Do you tremble to strengthen my resolve,
Or to terrify me?
Dear, sorrowful ashes, yes, I hear you whisper,
Yes, this bloody dagger will avenge the wrong done to you
To avenge you I was born.
It is done, I avenge you, and I in my turn die
But what do I see?]

It is obvious that Ducis' version only gives the slightest hint of Hamlet's original "To be or not to be," but from the French point of view this showed Shakespeare in a much more glorious light than could otherwise have been expected. The urn scene was the most popular element of the 1770 edition. One can see from reading Ducis' rewritten "To be" soliloquy that, while it remains a question of Hamlet building up the strength to strike against his father's murderer, this Hamlet is at once more classically heroic and more devoted in the bourgeois sense than the original.

Ducis' translations added immeasurably to the reputation of Shakespeare with the French public. A few purists, Diderot included, bewailed the loss of action compared to the original, but even he appreciated Ducis' easily flowing verses and the device of the urn.[11] Certainly the play was a tremendous hit with the public. Even though there is less blood, no humor, and no visible ghost, even though it was judged by prominent critics as lacking in action, the public appreciated the play's moral content and style. After the 1770 edition, the play went through another nine editions during Ducis' lifetime, and it was further reprinted in 1818, 1826, and even as late as 1830, the year of *Hernani* and the consecration of Romanticism. The play was acted twelve times in 1769–70 and a further 191 times between 1787 and 1851, all at the Comédie Française. Its record at that theatre is superior to that of any other tragedy written in the eighteenth century, with the exception of those written by Voltaire. The success of *Hamlet* was more than likely due to the fact that Ducis had presented a Shakespeare adapted to meet the expectations of the French public. This was, in short, a translation slanted toward the receiving culture, a completely acculturated translation. A pre-revolutionary eighteenth-century public expected to see an ending that would allow the hero to live to justify the action he had taken, and they also expected to be confronted with a familiar set of ideas and to have problems resolved before their eyes. For these reasons, Ducis' *Hamlet* appears to be perfectly in tune with the neo-classical ideals of the Académie Française. Should one look a little deeper, however, the motives underlying Ducis' translation of the play come to light.

Jürgen von Stackelberg has suggested that the tendency to view Ducis' *Hamlet* as a typical neoclassical adaptation of a foreign model, while not inaccurate, is to take the exterior, formal aspect of the play too seriously and to ignore certain thematic traits which echo the concerns displayed in eighteenth-century bourgeois domestic dramas.[12] The matricial changes Ducis made in Shakespeare's plot can almost all be put down to the ideology of the bourgeoisie. Hamlet is a tender, devoted son who shrinks before the task of murdering his mother; Gertrude overcomes her past lapses and rejects the advances of Claudius to protect her son; Ophelia, as a good daughter, at first takes the side of her father against her lover.

Ducis was, in fact, of bourgeois origin himself and was said to be a man of family values. His version of *Hamlet* received its premiere at the Comédie Française after several bourgeois dramas had ended their run elsewhere in Paris, among them a revival of Diderot's *Père de famille* and Surain's *Béverlei*. E. Preston Dargan's 1912 article, "Shakespeare and Ducis," notes two distinct infiltrations from such *comédies larmoyantes*, or "tearful" (sentimental) comedies.[13] According to Dargan, Ducis' *Hamlet* is composed of distinctly moralizing elements as well as being a faithful depiction of bourgeois *bienséance* – it is Shakespeare diluted with tears: "Everybody was more or less lachrymose and Ducis particularly so. Everybody wanted art to represent goodness after the order of Greuze; and the depiction of villains who may be admirable 'au fond'."[14]

Dargan also points out how often Ducis refers to the key word of bourgeois moralizing: "nature," and he finally classifies Ducis' *Hamlet* as a "drame de famille." In much the same way, Helen Phelps Bailey has characterized Ducis' Hamlet as follows: "Weak and effeminate, given easily to tears, he is *sensible* in the fullest eighteenth-century sense. Afflicted alternately by moods of mute depression and wild outbursts of terror, he anticipates René."[15]

Not only was Ducis' Hamlet a forerunner of Chateaubriand's seminal Romantic hero, the sensitive René; he also embodied the very essence of the bourgeois heroes of Diderot and Saurin. In addition to the play's evident neoclassical organization one can distinguish an eighteenth century concern for the sentimental, the somber, and the lachrymose throughout. This is not surprising, given the general state of the theatre in 1769. The audience of Ducis' *Hamlet* would, in the previous few years, have been used to seeing all manner of bourgeois plays. In 1765 the most popular play in France was Sédaine's *Le Philosophe sans le savoir*, closely followed by De Belloy's acclaimed historical drama *Le Siège de Calais* (which was of course lifted due to the efforts of the "burghers" commemorated in Rodin's celebrated sculpture). Beaumarchais, too, had been filling the theatres with plays such as his 1767 *drame Eugénie*, but the Comédie Française proved itself to be so resistant to this kind of play, which threatened the tenure of classicism, that the only way to have a bourgeois *drame* played there was to dress it up as a classical tragedy.

As we have seen, Ducis' *Hamlet* has the exact exterior shape of a classical tragedy, but it is also possible to find in it the *tendresse filiale* so beloved of the bourgeois. Hamlet is a pale, sensitive intellectual hero who hesitates to kill his mother because of his respect for the family hierarchy. Claudius portrays the young man as someone who is not fit to rule:

un foible Roi qui ne peut gouverner,
Une ombre, un vain phantôme inhabile à l'Empire,
Que consume l'ennui, que la mort va détruire.
                                        (I, i, 84–6)

[a weak king unable to govern,
A shadow, a shallow ghost, incapable of wielding influence,
Consumed by boredom, whom death will destroy.]

Later, however, one sees a Hamlet who can literally roar with imperiousness when freed of the constraints of filial piety. He addresses Claudius as follows:

> Tremblez, audacieux, de devenir rebelle,
> Avez-vous oublié que je suis votre Roi?
> (III, iii, 910–11)

> [Tremble, villain, for your treason
> Do you forget that I am your king?]

But for the most part these "manly" tones are exceptions. Most often Hamlet appears terrified of the wrath of his father, the Ghost, who materializes every time he closes his eyes. In the words of his friend, Norceste:

> Mes bras l'ont arrêté fuyant dans les ténèbres,
> Tremblant, pâle, égaré, poussant des cris funèbres.
> (II, iii, 481–2)

> [I caught him fleeing in the darkness
> Shivering, pale, distraught, howling mournfully.]

What he perceives as his duty to his father, the murder of his mother, puts him in a terrible dilemma which almost ends in his suicide. Hamlet's state of mind at this juncture is represented graphically by the "To be or not to be" monologue, directed to the ashes of the late king, present onstage in an urn. The tableau created by Talma, onstage, gazing imploringly at the urn, neatly symbolizes the *pietas filialis* which is at the root of the bourgeois psyche. The urn proceeded to tremble and groan in reaction to Hamlet's speech, which provoked the latter to declaim: "Cendre plaintive et chère, oui, j'entends ton murmure!" (IV, iii, 1108) [Dear, sorrowful ashes, yes, I hear your whisper.]

Just before this scene Hamlet had made a statement of bourgeois orthodoxy: "Ma gloire est d'être fils" (III, v, 995) [My glory is won through being a son], and to Ophelia he declares:

> On remplace un ami, son épouse, une amante,
> Mais un vertueux père est un bien précieux
> Qu'on ne tient qu'une fois de la bonté des Dieux.
> (III, v, 1047–9)[16]

> [A friend, a wife, a lover can be replaced,
> But a virtuous father is a precious possession
> That one is only given once through the grace of the Gods.]

Ducis' *Hamlet* is nothing more than a reflection here of Diderot's *Fils naturel*, the upholder of bourgeois family virtues. Despite all the turmoil in which he finds himself, and the terrible revelations he has faced, Hamlet still finds time to remember what a good educator his father was:

> Par quels soins assidus, avec quelle tendresse,
> Ce Père infortuné cultiva ma jeunesse!
> (II, v, 512–13)

> [With what unremitting care, how tenderly
> This wretched father oversaw my youth.]

Neither Shakespeare's Hamlet, nor Racine's Orestes – or even Corneille's Rodrigue ever spoke of his father in this way. Hamlet has been turned into a bourgeois.

Gertrude, too, appears as a model of chaste repentance. Her role is transformed to the point where she appears to be the very upholder of the *status quo*:

> Si par un crime affreux je l'ai privé d'un père,
> Il est bien juste au moins qu'il retrouve une mère.
> (I, ii, 297–8)

> [If through a horrible crime I have deprived him of a father
> It is only right that he should regain a mother.]

Her transformation from murderer into the best assurance of the continuation of the Hamlet dynasty is explained by Ducis in terms of Nature: one cannot escape one's identity and to whom one is related. In the best tradition of the times, Gertrude's maternal instincts shine through:

> prête à commettre un si grand parricide,
> La Nature en secret malgré nous s'intimide.
> (II, i, 402)

> [On the point of committing such a great parricide
> Our nature, despite itself, intimidates us.]

Her maternal nature is what finally makes her break with Claudius; her moment of excess is deeply regretted:

> Et la Nature exprès, pour mieux percer mon coeur,
> Jusqu'en mon propre sein s'est cherché son vengeur.
> (II, i, 435–6)

[And Nature deliberately, the better to pierce my heart,
Sought out her avenger within my own breast.]

Norceste conceives of "nature" in much the same way:

> J'admire ces regrets que la nature inspire:
> C'est de la voix du sang le légitime empire.
> (II, v, 509–10)

[I admire these regrets which nature inspires
It's the legitimate influence of blood.]

That is, blood is thicker than water.

In the same way that Gertrude's family ties prompt her to abandon Claudius, Hamlet's respect for his mother, even though somewhat weakened, will not allow him to kill her. Ducis would have drawn these sentiments of family and filial piety from a number of readily available sources, more likely eighteenth century than classical. A clue to his thinking lies in the fact that he prefaces his 1770 translation of *Hamlet* with a motto from Rousseau's *La Nouvelle Héloïse*:

> Accablée d'une si cruelle perte, mon âme n'eut plus de force que pour la sentir, la voix de la Nature gémissante étouffa les murmures de l'Amour.

> [Overwhelmed by such a cruel loss, my soul had only enough strength to feel that loss, the voice of groaning nature smothered love's murmurs.]

This comes from Julie's letter to Saint-Preux, in which she tells him of her conversion on the way to the altar and her decision to give up her love out of a sense of duty to her father, and to go back to her family. Both Gertrude's and Hamlet's subordination to the laws of family ethics at the expense of passion derives from Rousseau's thoughts on the family. The royal family of Denmark, in Ducis' play, represents not so much the Greek Atridae as that of Rousseau's M. de Wolmar.[17]

Hamlet thus appears before his mother, to force her to confess to her crimes over the ashes of his dead father. Faced with the urn, she cannot lie and falls faint, but neither can Hamlet kill her. His obligation to his father will be fulfilled if he kills Claudius (who is the only one actually guilty of regicide, since Gertrude was only a co-conspirator). This enables Ducis to echo the plot of *Le Cid*, with Ophelia/Chimène as the dutiful daughter giving up her love to side with her father. Admittedly this is classical material, but it was material the bourgeoisie had incorporated into their own code of ethics. Ophelia and Hamlet in the end both fulfill their duties to their parents, and all three parents are dead by the end of the play, but contrary to Shakespeare and Corneille, Ducis felt bound to provide a happy ending. Having fulfilled their duty, Hamlet and Ophelia are free to love each other, and the assumption is that they live happily ever after as king and queen (for even the bourgeoisie upheld the idea of a monarchy). This could also explain the fact that *Hamlet* went through a second successful period during the Restoration, before being replaced by the Dumas–Meurice translation.

It could be argued, then, that Ducis had a greater impact on the French theatre than is generally realized. His completely acculturated version of *Hamlet* allowed him to present a foreign play as a model of neoclassicism and introduce bourgeois drama into the Comédie Française by the back door, using the name *Hamlet* to gain access to the hallowed stage in a way a bourgeois *drame* could never have done. It would never have been possible for him to do the same using a French original – *Phèdre* could never be touted as a model of bourgeois ideology. Ducis' translation process largely reflects a code-abiding activity in that it preserves the neoclassical French tragic model. However, his translation decisions also introduce innovative themes since *Hamlet* uses elements of a non-canonized genre, the bourgeois melodrama, which had been rejected by the literary milieu of the Comédie Française as lacking in aesthetic value while remaining wildly popular on the boulevards, where traditionally most French theatrical innovation has taken place. By means of a manipulative rewriting of a foreign classic, Ducis managed to circumvent the Comédie Française's traditional resistance to new forms of drama.

Another explanation for the continued success of Ducis' translation is his friendship with the leading interpreter of Hamlet, the actor Talma. In much the same way as Mounet-Sully would later assume the persona of Hamlet to play the Dumas–Meurice translation, Talma assumed the character of the prince in Ducis' version. Talma knew English well, having spent a good deal of his youth in England, and studied the original to suggest revisions in the plot to Ducis, who did not know English. Indeed Talma used his position as one of the most influential *sociétaires*, or shareholders, at the Comédie Française to urge Ducis to mold the play to his (Talma's) own satisfaction. Talma's wish was to restore more and more of the scenes originally omitted by Ducis, thereby introducing a more plot-based translation of *Hamlet* and altering Ducis' matricial norms so that the dialogic structure of the translation came closer to that of the original – which thereby undermined Ducis' attempts to make the play a bourgeois drama. Between 1803, when Talma had briefly played the role of Hamlet (replacing Molé) at the Théâtre de la Porte Saint-Martin, until the play was printed as part of the complete works of Ducis in 1813, *Hamlet* was in a constant state of rewriting. The correspondence between Ducis and Talma bears witness to this, as do the numerous annotated copies of the text (in the hand of both men) to be found in various libraries. At Talma's request, Ducis wrote a whole new fifth act. On 29 *vendémiaire* in the year XII (October 22, 1803) Ducis wrote to Talma:

> In the fifth act, I gave full flight to my heart and my imagination. I wanted it to seem beautiful and to produce a fearsome effect worthy of tragedy. Let's quickly decide on the manuscript and then, please play my Hamlet. Please send me your thoughts as soon as possible.[18]

Between them they worked on a final scene which would enable Talma to bask in his genius for poetic discourse: "The rant must be flawless in style and it must recall Dante in imagery and color."[19]

Talma was not happy with the scope of Ducis' efforts and proceeded to ask him to "correct" the first four acts as well, plus a further revision of the fifth. Ducis was extremely receptive to Talma's requests (since by this time he was interested in extending the run of his play), one of which was the addition of "Mourir, dormir, rêver peut-être" ("To die, to sleep, perchance to dream") to the "To be or not to be" monologue now situated in IV, i. Talma had even invited Ducis to stay with him in the country so they could work on the all-important fifth act together. In 1806 Ducis once again submitted his work for the approval of the *sociétaires* at the Comédie Française. His *Hamlet* had last been performed in 1803, on three occasions, and before that in 1787, and before it could be played there again he would have to amend it to the satisfaction of the players, especially Talma. He wrote in the following suppliant manner:

> I know you are well disposed toward putting my tragedy *Hamlet* back in the repertory with all the changes and the new fifth act I added before I succumbed to this fever which has been eating away at me for the last three months. For eighteen months now I've been hoping that the work I've done on my manuscript might possibly be of use to you somewhere in your repertory. My illness prevents me from coming to see you to impress upon you my desire to see my tragedy in its new splendor.[20]

Still Talma insisted upon further modifications. In 1807 Ducis wrote to him:

> This morning I reread my new act of *Hamlet* which I copied out yesterday. It seems to me that it is made to the same recipe as the small morsel you already fed the public. I seasoned it as well as I could with grace, pity, and above all terror.[21]

Talma and the other *sociétaires* finally approved Ducis' modification of the play in line with their recommendations, which entailed the expansion of the role of Gertrude, and more blood on the stage. The tragedy was revived in this form on May 23, 1807, and from then it remained in the repertory of the Comédie Française until 1851, being modified occasionally to conform to political fluctuations. From his initial portrayal of Hamlet in 1803 at the Théâtre de la Porte Saint-Martin, until his death in October 1826, Talma was the only interpreter of Hamlet at the Comédie Française (with the exception of three performances by Victor).[22] After Talma's death the profits generated by the play, which had been huge, went down somewhat. However, Ducis had endowed his *Hamlet* with the chameleon-like quality of adapting to fit its surroundings, and it again became wildly popular in the years immediately following 1830, when the Romantic revolution was at fever-pitch.

Ducis' translation benefited from the performances of several famous actors, from Molé (who created the part on the French stage), to Larive, who succeeded him in the 1787 production, to Talma from 1803 to 1826. Talma it was who ensured that the translation adhered more closely to the integrity of Shakespeare's dramatic text, while at the same time seducing the crowd with his rendition of the urn scene and his emphasis on Hamlet's acute fear of the Ghost. Dressed in a black silk costume, topped by a greatcoat lined with fur, with his dagger and black leather boots, Talma is the link between the original neoclassical verse translation of *Hamlet* and the Romantic local color brought out in the role by Dumas. Like Ducis', Dumas' translation would have to undergo many changes before it would be accepted by the Comédie Française, and like Ducis', Dumas' play would be rewritten at the insistence of another great interpreter of the prince of Denmark, the actor Mounet-Sully.

Chapter 2

Alexandre Dumas and Paul Meurice's *Hamlet, Prince de Danemark*
Translation as an exercise in power

By the year 1842, fully twelve years after Romanticism had become the dominant movement in French theatre with the production of Victor Hugo's *Hernani* at the Comédie Française, only one French translation of *Hamlet* had been produced on the Parisian stage – that of Ducis, albeit in several versions. Legend has it that Alexandre Dumas père was publicly lamenting the lack of a better stage production of the Shakespeare play, which had been in the repertory of the Comédie Française since 1770, when Paul Meurice disclosed that he had attempted to translate *Hamlet* himself, staying close to Shakespeare's English. After reading Meurice's rough linguistic version Dumas offered to retouch it professionally, and together they presented it in 1846 for consideration by the reading committee of the Comédie Française. The play was rejected "*à correction*" (subject to revision) shortly thereafter.[1]

Dumas père belonged to a generation of French Romantics who had been brought up on Ducis' *Hamlet*, but whose first real acquaintance with the work had come about through the touring English companies of Edmund Kean and Charles Kemble in the late 1820s. At that time there was a great literary debate raging in France between the conservative neoclassicists, who sought to cling to the Racinian model for tragedy, and the proponents of the fledgling Romantic school, fired by the admiration of Hugo and Stendhal for the liberation a Shakespearian tragic model offered from neoclassicist strictures pertaining to genre and language usage. The Romantics' enthusiasm prompted a rapturous reception for the touring English companies, and cleared the way for the Comédie Française to accept more progressively oriented Romantic plays into its repertory, including Dumas' own *Henri III et sa cour* (1829).

Both Stendhal's *Racine et Shakespeare* (1823–5), in which the novelist declared Shakespeare's plays to be more suitable dramatic models than those of Racine, and Hugo's *Préface de Cromwell* (1827) enabled the English touring companies led by Kemble in 1827 and Macready in 1828 to perform a version of Shakespeare more oriented toward the source culture than had previously been seen on a French stage. Hugo, for example, had called into question such neoclassical tenets as the unities of time and place, the strict separation of genres, and the concept that drama should "idealize nature," advocating instead a depiction of humanity's grotesque qualities as well as its sublime nature. Dumas wholeheartedly agreed with both Stendhal and Hugo, and despite the fact that he was not fluent in English, the deep impression these English productions made on him was the catalyst behind his desire to produce what he considered to be a more representative version of Shakespeare's work.[2] Dumas' preliminary norm – his choice of *Hamlet* as a play to render into French, was thus determined by at least two factors – the current vogue for Shakespeare, championed by the avant-garde, and his own experience of seeing an English production of *Hamlet* on a French stage. He had particularly admired Charles Kemble's portrayal of Hamlet, in a performance at the Odéon on September 11, 1827. With Harriet Smithson as Ophelia, the English players enthralled Dumas with the real flesh and blood passions of Shakespeare's original characters, underlining even more sharply the distinction between an English interpretation of the play and Ducis' more classical stereotypes. However, the English company had itself heavily adapted its Shakespeare to meet with French approval: the plot had been simplified – there were no references to Norway, no role for Fortinbras; whatever risked alarming the conservative French ear had been cut or toned-down – Ophelia's songs, Hamlet's bawdy comments; sub-plots or other episodes not relevant to the main thrust of the story had been pruned – Polonius' scene with Reynaldo, the digression on child actors, Horatio receiving Hamlet's letter, and so on. The dialogue, too, had been shortened, and important passages had been cut out in order to bring the playing time down to more acceptable levels: out went the prince's monologue after the actor's tale of the death of Pyrrhus, Hamlet's scene with Gertrude in her chamber, and the scene where Claudius tries to pray.[3]

Despite the alterations in dramatic structure, Dumas was profoundly affected by the depiction of Ophelia's madness, the graveyard scene, and a piece of stage business in which Ophelia held up a fan while watching the play within the play, allowing Hamlet (from behind her) surreptitiously to observe the king's reaction. For nineteen years, Dumas had dreamed of replacing Ducis' version of the play with a translation capable of recreating the *Hamlet* he had seen at the Odéon. When his play was received "*à correction*" by the Comédie Française, he withdrew it in a fit of pique.[4]

Yet there was more to the situation, and Dumas' motives, than the desire to replace Ducis' translation with one which more closely reflected a Romantic interpretation of Shakespeare's original. What moved Dumas to withdraw his and Meurice's translation was a question of power. Despite the fact that he had originally only been involved with Meurice's version of the play in order to retouch it, Dumas nevertheless felt personally insulted by the Comédie Française's refusal to embrace it, and promptly resolved to have it played. Indeed one could see Dumas' annoyance with the old-style Comédie Française reading committee as a sign of the times. This august institution, despite having admitted Romantic plays to its repertory in the late 1820s, was still organized in much the same way as it had been when Racine was alive. The actors, and some critics, were still of the opinion that art should idealize rather than copy life. Thus the acting was still of the neoclassical "teapot" or declamatory variety, whereby the actor delivering the speech stood at the front of the stage and declaimed his or her lines to the audience, while the rest of the actors onstage stood behind, in a semicircle. When the play called for dialogue, there was considerable movement up and down stage, in and out of the full view of the audience, depending on whose turn it was to speak. The actors did not interact, but declaimed to the audience, eyes front. When Hugo staged *Hernani*, he borrowed heavily from melodrama in using the entire stage for the action, and even had actors turn their backs to the audience. He made them speak to each other, as if they actually believed in the plot, and the focus was thus shifted away from beautifully executed alexandrines to the story. The *sociétaires* at the

Comédie Française had previously decided on the *mise en scène* themselves, and were even known to perform encores, repeating speeches out of context when the audience applauded their delivery. Prior to *Hernani*, these *sociétaires* had control over almost every aspect of staging a play; in 1847, however, Dumas saw no need to accept that a troupe of actors knew how to write or direct a play. With his *Hamlet* translation he was attempting to force the pace of change at the Comédie Française: he sought to override the authority of the *sociétaires* and introduce the boulevard techniques of the immensely successful melodrama in which, ever since Pixerécourt in the early 1800s, power had rested with the playwright/director and the focus had been on the spectacle, on the story, rather than on the actors' ability to articulate beautiful dodecasyllables. Dumas, not unlike Ducis, attempted to use the translation of a classic play to impose an avant-garde model at the Comédie Française: in this case a model which afforded the playwright/director the power of veto over the *sociétaires*.

Dumas was not one to concede a point quietly. He hired a theatre in Saint-Germain-en-Laye, and presented his version of *Hamlet* to an invited audience of critics and celebrities, who were sufficiently moved by this *Hamlet*'s difference from the Ducis version to initiate a literary backlash, in numerous *feuilletons* and periodicals, against the theatrical philistines who had rejected it.[5] While their general argument had it that this *Hamlet* was more "faithful" to the original version than that of Ducis, on closer examination the Dumas–Meurice translation reveals itself to be less respectful of the English codes than one might expect. The initial norm to which Dumas adheres seems to have been brought about by his exposure to Shakespeare's original as performed by the English actors in Paris. But it will soon become apparent that he only kept certain interesting scenes from that production and that he molded Meurice's target language-oriented translation after his own notions of a popular romantic melodrama. Needless to say, Shakespeare's original was again acculturated and largely reflected traits of theatrical genres popular in Dumas' time and represented by his own works.[6]

As was mentioned above, Dumas' initial impressions of *Hamlet* had been based on largely "bowdlerized" English versions of the play, not on the integral text. His subsequent rewriting of Meurice's original translation resulted in a five-act play, in verse, which both added to and deleted from the original. Nevertheless, he restored to the play enough of its original features to hold the audience of the Théâtre Historique (where it was performed in public, as opposed to before a specially invited audience, for the first time in 1847) spellbound by the sight of skulls on stage, and a Ghost which appeared behind a wire curtain (as opposed to Ducis' Ghost which remained inside Hamlet's head and materialized only in the form of the ashes present in the urn).[7] The production was declared a popular success, which justified Dumas' belief in *Hamlet*'s capacity to be canonized and popularized in France.[8]

Yet Dumas' melodramatic adaptations did not sit so well with Meurice, who was quietly disturbed by certain matricial and textual modifications the former had made to his original linguistic translation in an attempt to force a melodramatic model into the Comédie Française. Hamlet, for example, does not die at the end of Dumas' play. Using a device familiar to readers of earlier English revenge tragedies, and thereby rendering the play more logical in its entirety to a French audience not used to seeing its heroes die, at least in melodrama, the Ghost of Hamlet *père* becomes visible to all of the other characters. Appearing as a *deus ex machina*, the Ghost acts as judge of Laertes (who dies, but is forgiven), Gertrude (who is advised to repent and seek forgiveness in Christ, and who also dies), Claudius (who dies after being damned), and Hamlet (who for his hesitation, and for having killed four people instead of one, is condemned to live). Had Hamlet died, reasoned Dumas, a French audience would have had trouble accepting the play since they expected strict, poetic justice to be meted out. Despite Meurice's objections, this was the version of his original translation performed by the actor Rouvière in subsequent revivals of the play at the Gaîté and the Odéon in 1855, after Rouvière had become so obsessed with the character of Hamlet that he virtually ceased to play any other role, finding inspiration for the part by surrounding himself with Delacroix paintings of Hamlet and the Ghost.[9]

The version of *Hamlet* performed at the Théâtre Historique had four different sets of scenery and was represented in seven tableaux. Further cuts were made to the play by Dumas in order to keep scene changes to a minimum and to make sure that the story remained as straightforward as possible.[10] The play progressed as follows.

Act I, first tableau (Scenes i–iv). The curtain rises, revealing not the ramparts of Elsinore, but the throne room. The second scene of Shakespeare's original is played out as normal, but the allusions to Norway are cut (and indeed Fortinbras does not figure in the play at all). As for Laertes, he comes back from France instead of asking to go there, all of which simplifies the plot along linear melodramatic lines, where an episodic story builds to a strong conclusion resulting in justice for all, and is written in an unequivocal moral tone, easily understood by everyone, not just the literary elite of the Comédie Française or the Romantic school.

Scene v has been invented by Dumas. The prince is alone, coming to terms with Horatio's tale of the Ghost, but cheers up immensely when Ophelia arrives on the scene. He writes her a note (which turns out to be the same one Polonius reads to Claudius and Gertrude in II, ii of Shakespeare) which is intercepted in Scenes vi and vii by Laertes, who then takes his sister to task. Since Laertes is not going anywhere, the father/son advice scenes have been cut.

The second tableau has four scenes corresponding to I, iv and v of the original. The Ghost appears to Hamlet on the ramparts, but there is no scene change since Hamlet tells Horatio and Marcellus to withdraw, remaining onstage with the Ghost.

The action of the second act all takes place in one room, within the castle, its seven scenes following Shakespeare II, i and ii. There is no scene between Polonius and Laertes, which detracts from the development of the father's character, but the former reappears in Act III plotting with Claudius to spy on Hamlet and Ophelia.

Dumas' version amalgamates Shakespeare's II, ii (420 ff.) and III, ii (1–53), the arrival of the actors with Hamlet's advice to them. It then takes Hamlet forty-five lines to outline the actor's art, and just ten for the actor to narrate the misfortunes of Hecuba.

In the second part of Act III of this adaptation, corresponding to III, ii (56 ff.) of Shakespeare, the scene commences with Hamlet confiding in Horatio, since the advice to the actors had come earlier. In the "Mousetrap" scene, the stage business admired by Dumas at Kemble's Odéon *Hamlet* is repeated – Hamlet watches Claudius and Gertrude from behind Ophelia's fan, and then crawls around on the floor (as did Kemble and later Macready), when Lucianus prepares to administer the poison to the sleeping Gonzago (dropped onto the lips, not into the ear).[11]

Hamlet's missed opportunity to slay the praying Claudius was dropped from this 1847 version, and (as in Ducis) instead of Hamlet going to Gertrude's bedroom, the queen comes to her son. The change is explained in the following terms by Hamlet:

> Dans sa chambre! oh! non pas!
> Car, là, l'époux vivant viendrait peut-être entendre,
> Ou l'époux mort troubler un entretien si tendre.
> (p.224)

> [Her bedroom? Oh, not there
> Since the living husband might perchance overhear
> Or the dead husband may disturb such a tender conversation.]

The prince does still kill Polonius, and once this is done the play moves swiftly toward a conclusion. Act IV begins with an echo of the suppressed prayer scene, where Claudius states his remorse, but this time for an explicit reason: the death of Polonius makes him reflect upon his crimes.

Act IV, Scenes i–iv of Shakespeare's play are then put aside – in the original, Polonius' murder is discovered, the body found, Hamlet arrested and sent to England. Yet Dumas' translation shows nobody apparently acting upon the death of Polonius (again a plot simplification). Gertrude, having seemingly given in to her son's entreaty not to sleep with Claudius, sees the king and tells him of Hamlet's flight from the scene when she spotted him hovering around the place where Claudius had been praying. Gertrude then asks for an assurance of Hamlet's safety, to which request Claudius is non-committal. In any case, Hamlet is neither arrested nor sent out of the country.

The next four scenes cover Shakespeare's IV, v–vii, with the omission of vi – Hamlet's letter to Horatio – due to the fact that Hamlet has not left the country. Ophelia's madness and subsequent death follow the original quite closely, as does Laertes' development of a plan to kill Hamlet. Ophelia's songs before her death have, however, been rendered decent for French ears. Where Shakespeare has the following (IV, v, 46–51):

> OPHELIA. Pray let's have no words of this, but when they ask you what it means, say you this:
> [*Sings*] Tomorrow is Saint Valentine's day,
>   All in the morning betime
>   And I a maid at your window
>   To be your Valentine.

Dumas at first follows the linguistic material quite closely, breaking the pattern of alexandrines with a sestet (IV, iii, p.239):

> OPHELIE. Nous n'allons plus parler de tout cela, j'espère!
>   Le sens caché? Mon Dieu! Je vais vous l'aplanir!
>   Voici le matin
>   De Saint Valentin
>   Et je viens, mutine,
>   Vous dire bonjour
>   Pour être ce jour
>   Votre Valentine!

> [We're not going to speak any more of this, I hope!
> What does it mean? My God, I'll spell it out for you!
>   This morning is Saint Valentine's day
>   And I have come, mischievously
>   To bid you good day
>   And to be this day your Valentine!]

However, when Shakespeare's Ophelia continues thus (IV, v, 52–5):

> Then up he rose and donned his clothes,
>   And dupped the chamber door;
> Let in the maid, that out a maid,
>   Never departed more.

Dumas omits this part of Ophelia's speech altogether and goes on to substitute the following sestet (IV, iii, p.239):

> "Bel ange adoré,
>   Je t'épouserai,"

>   Disiez-vous naguère.
>   Oui, mais, entre nous,
>   L'amant à l'époux
>   Fait trop peur, ma chère.
>
> ["My sweet, beloved angel
>   I will marry you"
> You said not long ago.
>   "Yes, but between the two of us
> The lover is too afraid of becoming
> The husband, my dear."]

for Ophelia's final song (IV, v, 59–66):

> By Gis and by Saint Charity,
>   Alack, and fie for shame!
> Young men will do't if they come to't.
>   By Cock, they are to blame.
>
> Quoth she, "Before you tumbled me,
>   You promised me to wed."

He answers:

> "So would I ha' done, by yonder sun,
>   An thou hadst not come to my bed."

The cemetery scene at the beginning of Act V is played out in its entirety, complete with the gravediggers' jokes, in keeping with the Romantic taste for depiction of the sublime and the grotesque. Shakespeare's V, ii to the end, is situated in the throne room. Guildenstern, who by now is dead in the original, returns as the king's messenger in place of Osric, to issue Hamlet the challenge to a duel. The swordplay was apparently effected with great panache by the actors concerned in the 1847 production[12] (again an element of melodramatic spectacle) and led to the final surprise reserved by Dumas for the audience (and Meurice). As already stated, the Ghost reappears when Claudius drinks from the poisoned chalice. The king, who does not see the Ghost at first, orders all the courtiers (including Horatio) to leave when he realizes he is dying, and as soon as they have left he sees the Ghost as also do Hamlet and, in the midst of their death throes, Gertrude and Laertes.

Hamlet remains alive at the end of this contrived scene of Dumas' own invention, a melodramatic finale to the play which ensures that only the guilty are punished. Dumas has the Ghost dispatch Laertes, then Gertrude, then Claudius (all of whom have drunk from the poisoned chalice), with the following lines:

> LAERTE [*au Fantôme*]. Grâce!
> LE FANTÔME.   Oui, ton sang trop prompt t'entraîna vers
>   l'abîme,
> Laërte, et le Seigneur t'a puni par ton crime.
> Mais tu le trouveras, car il sonde les coeurs,
> Moins sévère là-haut. Laërte, – prie et meurs!
>
> [*Laërte meurt*
>
> LA REINE. Pitié! pitié!
> LE FANTÔME.   Ta faute était ton amour même.
> Ame trop faible, et Dieu vous aime quand on aime!
> Va, ton coeur a lavé sa honte avec ses pleurs.
> Femme ici, reine au ciel, Gertrude, – espère et meurs!
>
> [*Gertrude meurt*
>
> LE ROI. Pardon!
> LE FANTÔME.   Pas de pardon! Va, meurtrier infâme!
> Pour tes crimes hideux, dans leurs cercles de flamme,
> Les enfers dévorants n'ont pas trop de douleurs!
> Va, traître incestueux! va! – désespère et meurs!
>
> [*Claudius meurt*
>
> HAMLET. Et moi? vais-je rester, triste orphelin, sur terre,
> A respirer cet air imprégné de misère?
> Tragédien choisi par le courroux de Dieu,
> Si j'ai mal pris mon rôle et mal saisi mon jeu,
> Si, tremblant de mon oeuvre et lassé sans combattre,
> Pour un que tu voulais, j'en ai fait mourir quatre, –
> Est-ce que Dieu sur moi fera peser son bras,
> Père? et quel châtiment m'attend donc?
> LE FANTÔME.   Tu vivras!
>
> (pp.267–8)

> [LAERTES [*to the Ghost*]. Have mercy!
> GHOST. Yes, your hot temper has pushed you to the brink of
>   the abyss,
> Laertes, and God has punished you for your crime.
> But you will find Him less severe in Heaven,
> For He probes all hearts, Laertes, pray and die!
>
> [*Laertes dies*

THE QUEEN. Mercy! Mercy!
GHOST. Your error lay in your own heart.
Your soul is weak; God loves you when you love him!
Go now, your heart has cleansed itself of shame through
   tears.
A mere woman here, a queen in heaven, Gertrude, have hope
   and die!

[*Gertrude dies*

THE KING. Forgive me!
GHOST. I shall not! Away, wretched murderer!
For your hideous crimes, Hell itself holds too
Few torments in its circles of flame!
Go, incestuous traitor, go! Despair and die!

[*Claudius dies*

HAMLET. And what of me? Am I to remain, as a sad orphan, on
   earth?
To breathe this air heavy with misery?
If I played my role badly and missed my chance
If I hesitated before my task and tired without fighting
I caused four people to die for the one you wanted
Will God then bring down his wrath upon me,
Father? What punishment awaits me?
GHOST. You will live!]

In addition to the objections of Meurice, other notable critics such as Théophile Gautier declared their preference for the Shakespearian ending. Dumas prevailed over his critics, saying that the French public would never tolerate all the slaughter at the end. Meurice wrote the scenario for the dénouement having bowed to the wishes of Dumas, who polished the text, as with Meurice's first translation.[13] As is evident from the final scene of Dumas' *Hamlet* quoted above, Ducis' neoclassical alexandrines have been greatly modified. The play is still written in alexandrines, of course, but Dumas has made great use of split lines and enjambement to speed up the delivery of the dialogue, and to make the action more natural. Following the lead of Hugo, who had required that his actors talk to each other and not to the back row of the balcony, Dumas' split alexandrines place the translation firmly in the Romantic/melodramatic tradition. Emphasis is switched from the quality of the actor's delivery to the plot, which again shifts power into the hands of the plot coordinator, the director Dumas.

In 1864, however, despite Dumas' opposition, Meurice revised the text of the play and restored Shakespeare's original dénouement, with a view to having his *Hamlet* performed for the tercentenary of the birth of the playwright. His new translation paid more attention to the linguistic and textual codes active in the original, and was performed in December 1867, at the Gaîté Theatre, with a veteran actress from the Comédie Française, Mme Judith, in the leading role. It was an immense success with critics and public alike, which prompted Alexandre Dumas to attempt to argue, writing article after article on the subject promoting his (translation) poetics, that his dénouement was more logical and dramatic than Shakespeare's original.

Meurice's 1864 version restores several scenes to their initial place in the narrative, including the advice to the actors in III, ii, Hamlet sparing the life of the king in III, iii, and the arrival of Fortinbras at the end. The Ghost appears once more in I, i to Horatio and his companions, and the references to Norway are restored as well. However, for the purposes of this translation, Norway is making plans to invade Denmark, and Laertes is sent on a mission to Norway with Voltimand, to make peace. This trip is substituted for his original trip to France, and serves the purpose of amplifying the allusions to Norway, which ceases to have designs on Denmark and sends Fortinbras against Poland in II, ii. From this point, Meurice introduces an emphatic interpretative shift in characterization: Fortinbras is contrasted with Hamlet, as the man of action against the man of inaction, who is once more seen hesitating to kill Claudius. Meurice also restores the scenes following Polonius' death (IV, i–iii), during which Hamlet is arrested and sent to England. He does differ from Shakespeare, though, in that Hamlet defies the king's orders and refuses to be sent to England, at which point Claudius backs down. Also restored is Hamlet's meeting with the Captain of Fortinbras' army en route to Poland, which in Shakespeare precedes Hamlet's departure. Here, the meeting takes place near the graveyard where Hamlet, having taken refuge from the court, has arranged a rendez-vous with Horatio. This meeting now precedes the gravediggers' jokes, and the "Alas poor Yorick! I knew him, Horatio" speech (V, i in

Shakespeare). Finally Hamlet, before dying, recommends the election of Fortinbras to the throne of Denmark, and the latter has him buried with honors.[14]

The subsequent success of the play prompted Meurice to try once more to have it accepted by the Comédie Française, which had ceased to perform Ducis' version in 1851. After many years, he managed to secure a promise from the then manager of the Comédie Française, Emile Perrin, that he would produce the tragedy. It was by now 1883, and Dumas had been dead for thirteen years. Mounet-Sully, the leading man of the Comédie Française, desperately wanted to play the role of Hamlet, and argued forcefully that Perrin start rehearsing the piece. However, Perrin died and despite the objections of Mounet-Sully, his replacement, M. Claretie, and most of the *sociétaires* decided they could ill afford a failure at such a time, and promptly rejected Meurice's version once more. Mounet-Sully persisted in his entreaties, however, and the tragedy was finally put into rehearsal.[15]

Before his death, Perrin had said that he would only accept the text of *Hamlet* subject to certain modifications in the style and structure of Meurice's "faithful" 1864 translation. From now on the Ghost, which had been referred to as "le fantôme" was to be called "le spectre", and "Bautista" (queen of the players) was to be renamed "Baptista."[16] Evidence of the infighting at the Comédie Française emerges in that Meurice was asked to give the character of Laertes more nobility, presumably at the insistence of Raphaël Duflos, one of the *sociétaires*, who was to play the role.[17] After the substitution of Dumas' original "judgment" ending for Meurice's temporary restitution of the role of Fortinbras, thanks to the suggestions of Dumas fils who had taken over his late father's interest in the play, *Hamlet* was finally readmitted to the repertory of the Comédie Française on April 28, 1884.[18] However, as can be inferred from the above, Dumas' battle for artistic control had ended in failure with the *sociétaires* still very much in charge of the material.

Claretie asked Meurice for three supplementary tableaux, presumably to show off the fabulous costumes replete with fur and authentic "Danish" characteristics which he was having designed. The king's coat alone cost 5,000 francs, and was inspired by an Albrecht Dürer painting in a belated attempt by the Comédie Française to inject some Romantic "local color" into the play. It should be noted also that Claretie's production of *Hamlet* was now projected to compete directly with the Cressonnois–Samson translation at the Porte-Saint-Martin, starring Sarah Bernhardt as Ophelia. This production, in addition to drawing on Ms Bernhardt's star quality, was also to be lavishly costumed, in the style of the Middle Ages.[19] In other words, "exoticized" and "historicized" translations were the norm of the day.

Given the competition offered by the Porte-Saint-Martin, Meurice and Dumas fils collaborated to produce the translation which was finally performed at the Comédie Française on September 28, 1886.[20] This translation differs from Meurice's 1864 text in several respects. The invented love-letter scene between Hamlet and Ophelia (I, iii) now comes in I, ii, directly after Hamlet's first monologue, not immediately after he has heard from Horatio about the apparition of the Ghost. The Ghost now appears after the scene in which Laertes, and then Polonius, warn Ophelia not to be wooed by Hamlet's advances. Hamlet's advice to the first player has been restored to its original place, and no longer comes when he welcomes the actors to Elsinore, but is given immediately before "The Murder of Gonzago." The actor's reply about Priam's death and Hecuba's sorrow is restored to its original length. Once again, however, everything relating to Fortinbras has been deleted, along with the scenes which follow Polonius' murder in which Hamlet is arrested and brought before the king. Here the play reverts to the original Dumas scenario of the 1847 translation.

As to the role of Laertes, his nobility is developed as follows: when he comes back from Norway (retained from the 1864 edition) to learn of his father's death and his sister's madness, his desire for revenge has been suppressed. He reacts to Claudius' talk of the murder of Hamlet with disdain. It takes Ophelia's death to push him over the edge and seek the death of Hamlet by any means. The play ends with a dying Hamlet delivering the line, "Le reste est silence." Horatio remains silent and Fortinbras is nowhere to be seen. Meurice furnished his alternative ending (with Fortinbras), plus a list of all the corrections he had been required to make, in the actors' copies of the script, as if in silent protest.[21]

When this production was revived in 1896, Fortinbras had

been restored once again at the insistence of Mounet-Sully, who had been so taken with the role that he had researched it thoroughly with the help of François-Victor Hugo's 1859 prose translation.[22] The undimmed power of the *sociétaires* is illustrated by the fact that at Mounet-Sully's insistence, several rather idiosyncratic corrections were made to his role. For instance, Mounet-Sully took Rosencrantz, not Horatio, to be Hamlet's old friend in his concern to bring out the fact that Hamlet trusts the wrong people and to highlight his surprise when he finds out that Rosencrantz is working against him.[23] Perhaps the most telling evidence of Mounet-Sully's influence, however, was the eventual restoration at his insistence of the role of Fortinbras, and all the references to Norway to the text of the 1896 edition. This was not a decision solely born out of concern for the textual material of the original, but out of a *sociétaire*'s desire to see his role fleshed out. In the days before directors ruled the stage at the Comédie Française (after all Antoine had only just established the Théâtre Antoine), the major stars directed themselves. Mounet-Sully was of the opinion that Fortinbras provided him with an important counterpoint to his own character (action versus inaction), so he had Fortinbras incorporated into the *mise en scène*. Moreover, he also had the number of intervals reduced to four in an effort to speed up the playing time – which would also enable more scenes to be played.[24]

Although he could not effect all the changes he wished, Mounet-Sully nevertheless gave the Comédie Française *Hamlet* a tone closer to that of Shakespeare's dramatic text than its predecessors by relying on François-Victor Hugo's prose translation and the English original to reconstruct Hamlet's thought process, an aspect of the play to which Meurice and Dumas chose not to pay attention.[25] In this way Mounet-Sully portrayed Hamlet's madness as sometimes real, sometimes feigned, providing cues within the text for his adoption of certain postures: when he sees the king and Polonius hiding as he comes to meet Ophelia, the realization that she has betrayed him prompts him to put on his mask of madness for her, too, and causes the retort "Va t'en dans un couvent" ("Get thee to a nunnery" (III, i, 121)) to be delivered with great force.[26]

Mounet-Sully was such a success in the role that he carried on playing it until his death, taking it on his personal tours to the

United States and England after its run at the Comédie Française ended in 1897. His influence on the text was extraordinary, and he, too, prevailed on poor Meurice and the Calmann-Lévy publishing firm to incorporate the changes he made onstage into the printed edition of the text. In 1910, Mounet-Sully was indirectly responsible for a production of the Schwob–Morand translation of *Hamlet*, since Mounet-Sully had identified himself so completely with the Meurice translation that he would not allow anyone to understudy him. Consequently, when the Baron d'Estournelles de Constant asked permission of Claretie to play the text in another theatre, the latter advised him to use the Schwob–Morand translation instead.[27] In 1932, after the death of Mounet-Sully, the Comédie Française finally laid aside the Dumas–Meurice *Hamlet* in favor of the Schwob–Morand translation, *La Tragique Histoire d'Hamlet*.

The early history of *Hamlet* in France, then, can be seen in terms of a power game for artistic control over the translation and the establishment of new literary models into the French canon. Both Talma and Mounet-Sully used their power as *sociétaires* to alter the translation to their wishes, to give themselves more prominence; Dumas used the translation to win more power for himself as artistic director by installing a melodramatic model which gave less prominence to the actors despite Meurice's silent protests in favor of the source text, and Ducis used the translation to undermine the Comédie Française's neoclassical repertory in favor of the bourgeois "drame."

Chapter 3

Marcel Schwob and Eugène Morand's *La Tragique Histoire d'Hamlet*
A folkloric prose translation

In 1899, at the height of the "Belle Epoque," large crowds flocked to a Parisian theatre to witness the inauguration of a new translation of *Hamlet*, by Marcel Schwob and Eugène Morand, starring Sarah Bernhardt in the role of the prince. The idea of casting a woman as Hamlet was not new: it had already been done in England, where the tradition of drag in pantomime had been established by Augustus Harris at Drury Lane in the 1880s, making the sight of a woman in the role of a "principal boy" and a man playing the "dame" not at all uncommon. There had even been a female Hamlet in France, thirty-two years previously, in 1867, when Dumas authorized Mme Judith to play the role in the Gaîté production of Meurice's revised translation of the play. Dumas noted that the play was a great success, and that Mme Judith took three curtain calls.[1] It was no great surprise therefore that the Schwob–Morand translation proved to be a huge success, given the immense drawing-power of Sarah Bernhardt. What was striking about this particular *Hamlet* was that it combined box-office appeal with iconoclasm – it was the first prose version of *Hamlet* ever to be played on the French stage.

Sarah Bernhardt had already played several more "orthodox" Shakespeare roles – indeed one of the first plays that brought her to public attention was Jules Lacroix's translation of *King Lear* in 1868 at the Odéon, where she scored a major triumph as Cordelia. Ten years later she played Desdemona opposite Mounet-Sully at the Comédie Française in a reportedly lukewarm version of Vigny's translation of *Othello*; her two Lady Macbeths met with critical indifference in Paris and London in

1884, and her 1886 Ophelia also failed to bring her recognition as a great Shakespearian actress.

Christopher Smith has made the observation that she never played the kind of roles "which a leading English actress might have expected to have the opportunity of interpreting," such as Juliet, Portia, and the heroines of the romances, noting that she had, moreover, "always played Shakespeare in versions substantially refashioned for the French stage."[2] Perhaps this is what inspired Bernhardt to take on the greatest of Shakespearian roles in a version of the text which she believed would finally allow her to represent the true complexity of an Elizabethan hero, for she considered Schwob's translation to be far more attentive to the original than any of its predecessors. She accepted the role in the wake of her performance in 1896 as Musset's Lorenzaccio (in the play of the same name), a role similar to Hamlet in that young Lorenzo is a model of temperamental incapacity for action (a quality which, according to Bernhardt, would be brought out perfectly by a woman). She had proved herself to be something of a risk-taker by accepting the challenge of taking on the role of Lorenzo, since Musset's closet drama had previously been considered unplayable, because of its numerous changes of scenery and tone and its inherent violence. *Lorenzaccio* was the most Shakespearian French Romantic drama (and one of the longest), and it proved to be the perfect launching pad for this *Hamlet*, due to the attention Bernhardt received when she staged it, since the public accepted her in a psychologically complex role, in a long, though action-packed, play.

Although *Hamlet* had been played in France for over a hundred years, in Bernhardt's eyes the French public had only been presented with partial plots, different characterization, and verse forms quite unlike those contained in the original. Her success in the role of Lorenzaccio had proved to her that it was possible to perform a long, violent, and "unplayable" text on the French stage with some degree of success. Her resultant eagerness to tackle a great Shakespearian role in what she considered to be its "unadulterated" form, and Schwob and Morand's willingness to provide her with the source text oriented translation she sought, would drastically change the way the French looked at theatre. The production was intended to remain closer to the narrative structure and vital imagery of

Shakespeare's *Hamlet* than any translation that had previously been performed in French.

Guaranteed an audience, and a star who was interested in staging a source text oriented translation, Schwob and Morand set about their task. Unlike Ducis and Dumas, Schwob was bilingual in French and English; he did not have to use an intermediary translation, as Ducis had used La Place and Dumas Meurice. In his preface to the play Schwob made it clear that he had produced a "new translation" of the complete text, not an adaptation.[3] The very fact that he felt the need to make this point should indicate how revolutionary a translation this would prove to be, in that Schwob was able to produce his translation entirely from the complete, unabridged source text. His goal was philological: he aimed to produce a translation based solely on linguistic criteria and textual analysis without being bound by French classical rules of prosody. Since his overriding interest was to capture the flavor and the imagery of Shakespeare's language, Schwob opted to translate in prose.

The decision to produce a prose Shakespeare was not taken lightly by Schwob or Morand; such a translation had been mooted in French literary circles as a response to what were perceived as the limitations of previous Shakespeare verse adaptations. In an 1895 article in the *Revue de Paris*, Maurice Bouchor had recommended that prose be used for Shakespeare's blank verse as well as his prose, "with French verse reserved for the passages in which rhyme is used in the original and for songs."[4] All these factors determined Schwob and Morand's translation policy as well as their initial norm, that is their attempt to stay as close as possible to the linguistic and textual/narrative codes active in Shakespeare's *Hamlet*. The only shift they announced was their decision to translate the play into prose.

Philippe van Tieghem has pointed out that although Shakespeare had been influential on French dramatic technique from 1850 onwards, and although this influence had even extended to prose fiction, it was only toward the end of the century that complete performances of his plays were risked onstage in Paris.[5] This is why the Bernhardt/Schwob/Morand version of *Hamlet* was so pivotal to the reception of Shakespeare in France: it proved to be a counterpoint to the poetic and cultural practices of both classicism and realism. Far from being the wish-fulfillment of a capricious star, this production of the integral text represents a vital stage in the assimilation of Shakespeare into French literary and theatrical tradition. Schwob and Morand were very serious about what they saw as their scholarly duty to introduce the real Shakespeare to the French. In their introduction to *La Tragique Histoire d'Hamlet*, they survey the pre-Shakespearian accounts of the play, stressing its French heritage in an attempt to "reclaim" *Hamlet* not only philologically but culturally, as they posit Old French literary models and practices as antecedents of Shakespeare's text.[6]

From the outset Schwob argued that *Hamlet* had a French source, perhaps in order to make his subsequent translation decisions more logical. Therefore, in the preface it is recorded that, during the thirteenth century, the chronicle of Saxo Grammaticus included the story of "Amlethus" in the third and fourth book of its *Danish History*. This chronicle was printed in 1514, and, in 1570, François de Belleforest translated the Hamlet story in the fifth book of his *Histoires tragiques*. In Schwob's opinion (p.ix), if Shakespeare used this version as his inspiration for *Hamlet*, then he must have read it in French, since the English translation of de Belleforest – *The Historie of Hamlet* – appeared in 1608, well after the first performance of Shakespeare's play.

In addition to de Belleforest, Schwob (p.x) refers to another possible source for *Hamlet*, suggested by Anatole France in the fourth volume of his *La Vie littéraire*, referring to collected tales published by Bladé under the title of *Contes populaires de la Gascogne*. Bladé had transcribed an oral tale called "La Reine châtiée," or "The Chastened Queen," which turns out to be a variant of the *Hamlet* legend, complete with a ghost, a prince who hesitates, then withdraws, before returning to fulfill the task required of him by the ghost, a Horatio figure, and a girl with whom Hamlet is in love and whom he sends to the convent. The only differences in the tale are the motive for the queen's murder of the king, and the absence of a Claudius figure. Schwob proceeds to link the Gascon folk tale to the original play, noting that Shakespeare also had his doubts about Gertrude's crime (pp.x–xiv). In the first version of *Hamlet* (the 1603 quarto) the queen is innocent of the poisoning: she does not know about it, and when Hamlet reveals the murder to her she becomes his ally. This is one of the main differences between the 1603 and 1604 versions emphasized by Schwob. His conjecture is that the 1603 quarto agrees with Kyd's *Ur-Hamlet*, and that the 1604 quarto is based, in part, on an oral legend, to which the Gascon tale bears witness (p.xv).

It should already be evident that Schwob's appraisal of the text differs widely from those of Dumas and Ducis, who did not really know the English language and who worked solely within the French literary and theatrical tradition to acculturate Shakespeare. Schwob, on the other hand, is so concerned with "fidelity" to the source text and scholarly exactitude that he is keen to contextualize his translation by providing his readers with the complete genealogy of the play as he sees it. Indeed, upon further examination of Bladé's anthology, Schwob suggests that the story of Hamlet is not the only Shakespearian legend preserved in Gascony. He asserts that a tale named "La Gardeuse de dindons" ("The Turkey Keeper") is closely related to *King Lear*. This oral legend contains the characters of Lear, Regan, Goneril, Cordelia, and Kent. The ending is different; it appears to be based on an intermediary type of story situated somewhere between *Peau-d'Ane* and *Cendrillon* (*Cinderella*). *Lear* and *Hamlet*, according to Schwob, therefore belong to thirteenth-century Anglo-Saxon folklore, and were originally brought to France by the English, taking root during the 300-year English occupation of Guyenne (p.xv).

The introduction proceeds from matters genealogical to a thorough textual analysis of Shakespeare's *Hamlet*, which highlights the translation process favored by Schwob. He reports that before completing his version of the play he examined the differences between the first (1603) quarto and the second (1604) quarto, paying particular attention to the Player King's address to the Player Queen (III, ii, 164-9). He points out that whereas he found the verses worthy of Shakespeare in the 1603 quarto, he considered them "full of gongorism" in the 1604 quarto, which caused him to wonder why Shakespeare replaced such beautiful verses by a "pompous and empty" stanza. Before translating the stanza, Schwob concluded that the actors had to stand out as distinct from the other characters: if the verses they uttered had been in the same style as the language of the rest of the play, there would have been a false perspective. Shakespeare accordingly did not hesitate to suppress this fragment of the first quarto to replace it quite intentionally by verse written in the manner of the Spanish poet de Gongora (1561–1627). The same holds true for the verse style of the "Murder of Gonzago," as well as for "The rugged Pyrrhus" monologue in which the style is marked by archaisms (pp.xvi–xviii).

The introduction continues in this vein, with Schwob's analysis of Hamlet's character, his madness (and Edgar Allen Poe's views on it, as expressed in the *Marginalia*), the role played by death, and exegetical clarifications of certain lines in the play.[7] After having devoted sixteen pages to scholarly interpretations of the drama and its origin, Schwob and Morand outline their translation practice. They emphasize that theirs is "une traduction de bonne foi" [in good faith], despite the Italian proverb ("traduttore traditore"), and most certainly not a commentary on the play (which is nevertheless provided in the introduction) (p.xxv). They claim to have represented words by words, and sentences by sentences. French critics had already accused Schwob and Morand of having gone out of their way to include archaisms in their *Hamlet*; the English had faulted them for having created too many neologisms. The introduction justifies their use of a more "archaic" vocabulary by stressing that the play needs to be translated into language current at its time of origin. Indeed, Schwob contended that there existed an analogy of languages and literatures at the same stage in their development; he believed that a language, having reached a certain stage in its evolution, should be translated into another language that had reached the same stage in its evolution: "One can hardly believe to what extent expressions and turns of phrase are analogous in two languages which have reached the same stage of their development."[8]

Schwob advises translators to translate texts not in contemporary language, but in the language of the period corresponding to that of the source texts to be translated.[9] He had already translated Catullus, a Latin poet of the first century BC, in the French of Clément Marot's time:

> It seemed to me that in Catullus' time, the Latin language had more or less developed to the same degree as the French language had done under Henri IV.... Moreover, this analogy can easily be explained in this case: in the sixteenth century, as under Caesar, the language of Greek literature was all-pervasive: one can recognize Greek in words and ideas. This

is why in my opinion, Catullus can only be translated into Old French.[10]

By applying this historicizing method, Schwob hopes to avoid the inherent shortcomings of verse translation: "Translations in verse have a bad reputation: either they preserve the form and change the meaning, or they preserve the meaning and send the form to the devil. The two methods are equally defective."[11] On the other hand, he claims that his historically rooted prose translations preserve both meaning and form.

In their translation, Schwob and Morand wish to emphasize that Shakespeare was writing during the reigns of Henri IV and Louis XIII. While aware that French verse cannot be an adequate substitute for English verse, they claim that their task is much like that of the engraver of a painting; whereas an engraver cannot capture the colors of the original, he or she will be able to capture its essence (p.xxvi). Schwob and Morand thus hope to "etch the radiant outline" of Shakespeare's creation: they see translation as a particular type of mimesis and recognize that it will be interpreted and adapted to a new medium, a new cultural language. They justify a number of their literal interpretations of individual lines of *Hamlet* in those terms. They translated, for example, "old mole" as "vieille taupe" and "wormwood" as "absinthe." To the English imagination these words evoke the "boulevard," its cafés, and its (female) passers-by. But, as Schwob and Morand stress, in French literature a mole is a mole, and "absinthe" remains a bitter plant. They go on to speculate that within a few years, when the "apéritif" is no longer in fashion and when French slang has changed, "taupe" and "absinthe" will signify their object *sub specie aeternitatis*, even in England (pp.xxv–xxvi).

In the notes following their introduction Schwob and Morand explain one of the most remarkable features of their translation. Their practice was to italicize any words they added to the text (even such seemingly uncontroversial words as "*ma* mère" for Hamlet's "mother," perhaps to retain the same number of syllables as the English) in an attempt to illustrate that they had produced a word-for-word translation. They further invite philologically inclined readers to compare their version of *Hamlet* with the text from which they worked, by naming their source as Edward Dowden's 1899 edition of the play.

Given the care with which they approached their task, it is not so very far-fetched to compare Schwob and Morand's translation practice with that of Bible translators. Their introduction, as well as their notes, point to thorough scholarly research. The notes following the translation refer to the source editions used to clarify several translation solutions. They also offer two appendices. One is an "Adaptation à la scène" in which cuts made for the Bernhardt stage production are indicated. The other is entitled "Quelques indications pour la mise en scène" and provides stage directions such as scenery to be used, a description of the stage, the exits and the positioning of various characters, the tone of voice actors should use in their lines, the gestures to be used by the actors, and the orchestration of the duel in the last act.

Given Schwob's theories of language, and the fact that he has chosen to translate *Hamlet* in the French of Henri IV's time, it is clear that his major objective was to preserve as much of a sense of Shakespeare's language as possible. This concern for using an historical French equivalent of Elizabethan English puts his text at odds with those of all other *Hamlet* translators, who, with the possible exception of Michel Vittoz, chose to use a form of French contemporary to their audience.

However, Jean-Claude Noël has somewhat discredited Schwob's claim to have written in the French of Henri IV by showing that, in addition to using seventeenth-century vocabulary, he also used a number of expressions normally associated with the Renaissance and even with the Middle Ages. For instance, the terms *féé* (bewitched), *rêver* (to think), and *admiration* (surprise) were used regularly in the seventeenth century. Similarly, the forms *occire* (to kill), *chef* (head), *nice* (naive, natural), *semblance* (resemblance), *cettui crâne* (this skull/head) and *quant à icelui sire* (as to that, my lord), although considered old and out-moded in Corneille's time, were still to be found in contemporary poetry and are therefore not out of place in Schwob's translation. Nevertheless, words like *caroles* (song), *fame* (renown), *moult* (a lot), *oignement* (ointment), *gabelleries* (very minutious exams), and *matagrabolisation* (dispute), while still used in Rabelais' time, properly belong to the lexicon of the Middle Ages. In other words, Schwob did not recreate in its entirety the French language of the beginning of the seventeenth century.[12] It may be true that the French linguistic codes

Schwob observes do not correspond to a specific period in time, but then language usage (*parole*) is not always fixed within a particular time frame either.[13] In rewriting *Hamlet* in the language of Henri IV, Schwob does not claim to have reconstructed that language *in toto*, but simply to have given the reader/spectator the illusion that he reconstituted it. It is enough (for him) to render the tone, to create the atmosphere, to make believe. The translation decisions made by Schwob with regard to language usage underline his concern with the time-bound elements of Shakespeare's original. In a manner following the "historicizing versus modernizing" axis discussed in the introduction, Schwob attempts to evoke both the historical flavor of the setting and the time-bound language usage of the original in his translated text, by selecting comparable historical (most often seventeenth-century French) solutions on the linguistic, literary, and socio-historical level. As James S Holmes has pointed out, a translator's choices need not be "all of a piece": a translation need not provide a complete set of seventeenth-century language alternatives to give the flavor of a Henri IV period piece.

Besides using archaisms to emulate Shakespeare's language, Schwob attempts to reflect Shakespeare's erudition and multiple referentiality in his use of specialized vocabulary: terms borrowed from administrative law, such as *duplique* (answer to a replique) and *triplique* (answer to the duplique), as well as terms taken from the register of jurisprudence, such as *susdit* (foresaid), *dessusdit* (aforementioned), *icelui* (the latter).[14] To approximate Shakespeare's tone, Schwob and Morand use expressions which vaguely recall certain epic conventions, such as the Homeric epithet: "L'Aube roulée dans son manteau roux passe sur la rosée de cette colline orientale" (p.13) ("The morn in russet mantle clad/ Walks o'er the dew of yon high eastward hill") (I, i, 167–8). Or they characterize a whole people with a summary characteristic feature: "Il abbatit sur la glace les Polonais meneurs de traîneaux" (p.10) ("He smote the sledded Polacks on the ice") (I, i, 63).[15]

Schwob attempted to stay close to Shakespeare's register whenever possible, translating the vulgar in concrete, graphic terms. He was quite aware that the main characters in *Hamlet* are nobles, who in French plays were expected to speak "nobly," but he chose to echo Shakespeare's tone at the risk of offending French ears. Whereas Dumas has already been seen to alter the tone of Ophelia's songs, Schwob renders them almost word for word:

> Demain c'est la Saint-Valentin;
> Fillette, dès matines,
> A votre fenêtre m'en viens:
> Suis votre Valentine.
> Lors se lève, puis lors s'habille;
> Lors la porte il ouvrit:
> Et de sa chambre la fille
> Plus fille ne sortit.
>
> Par l'Enfant, par la Charité!
> Hélas! oh, fi! la honte!
> Garçon y va s'il est tenté;
> Parbleu, c'est grand mécompte.
> "Avant de me trousser, fit-elle,
> Le mariage on me promit."
> *Il répond*:
> Par le jour, l'eusse fait la belle,
> Si tu n'avais cherché mon lit.
>   (pp.125–6)
>
> (Tomorrow is Saint Valentine's day,
> All in the morning betime,
> And I a maid at your window
> To be your Valentine.
>
> Then up he rose and donned his clothes,
> And dupped the chamber door;
> Let in the maid, that out a maid,
> Never departed more.
>
> By Gis and by Saint Charity,
> Alack, and fie for shame!
> Young men will do't if they come to't
> By Cock, they are to blame.
> Quoth she, "Before you tumbled me,
> You promised me to wed."
> *He answers*:

'So would I ha' done, by yonder sun,
An thou hadst not come to my bed.")
(IV, v, 48–66)

The Schwob–Morand *Hamlet* shows a remarkable propensity for choosing French words close to the English source text not only in meaning, but also in sound. The alliteration of consonants in Shakespeare's English is often echoed by vocalic assonance in Schwob and Morand's French. Shakespeare's III, i, 60–1: "and, by a *s*leep to *s*ay we end – The heart ache" (emphasis added), becomes: "et p*ar* un dorm*ir* se d*ire* que c'est la fin de l'angoisse du coeur" (p.75, emphasis added).

In many cases they transliterate rather than translate idiomatically, and arrange material so that it adheres to the word order of the source text

BERNARDO. Longue vie au roi! (p.7)
           (Long live the king) (I, i, 3).
HORATIO. C'en est un morceau (p.8)
           (A piece of him) (I, i, 19).
BERNARDO. Assieds-toi un temps (p.8)
           (Sit down awhile) (I, i, 30).

Schwob and Morand translate almost like a gloss, choosing to retain Shakespeare's exact imagery and vocabulary. For example, Shakespeare's (HAMLET.) "I am too much in the sun" (I, ii, 67) becomes "je suis trop près du soleil" (p.16). The doublets dropped by Ducis and Dumas–Meurice are preserved in Schwob's translation. Suffice it to quote: (HAMLET.) "l'attirail et le parement de la douleur" (p.17) ("the trappings and the suits of woe" (I, ii, 86)), along with "Oh, si cette trop, trop solide chair voulait se fondre" (p.18) ("O that this too too sullied flesh would melt" (I, ii, 129)). In fact, sometimes Schwob enlarges upon Shakespeare's doublets, in this case using a triplet: "que des choses *informes* [misshapen] fétides et grossières" (pp.18–19) ("Things rank and gross" (I, ii, 136)).

By remaining close to English word order, Schwob and Morand appear to have found it easier to uncover the syntactic forms of Old French. If one looks at Schwob's translation strategies closely, as Noël does, it appears that they are developed from the English and then repeated here and there in translation. For example, Schwob chose regularly to suppress the article. He translates: "Such an act/ That blurs the grace and blush of modesty" (III, iv, 41–2) as "Un acte tel qu'il ternit la grâce et rougeur de *modestie*" (p.103, emphasis added) and "the morn and liquid dew of youth" (I, iii, 41) as "la matinale et liquide rosée de *jeunesse*" (p.25, emphasis added). The use of such a strategy would appear to back up Schwob's claim to have used seventeenth-century French, since Noël points to a rule whereby in the seventeenth century omission of the article in front of a noun resulted in its personification.[16]

A second strategy used by Schwob to transpose what he considers the "integrity" of the text is the use of the adverbial adjective in French. Where Shakespeare wrote "the morning cock crew loud" (I, ii, 218), the translator transposed textually: "le coq du matin a chanté clair" (p.21). The use of adjectives having the value of adverbs originated in popular speech: grammarians admired such usage in the sixteenth century. Schwob, knowing this, applies a rule formulated at about the same time in which he situated his translation.[17]

A third procedure imitated from Shakespeare is the use of the obsolete ablative. Where the English playwright has: "their perfume lost,/ Take these [remembrances] again" (III, i, 99–100), Schwob translates: "*leur parfum perdu*, reprenez-les" (p.77, emphasis added). Again, as Noël remarks, modern French grammar permits such constructions, but in practice the French avoid them as much as possible, since they can hamper understanding because the ablative is not linked to the main clause in a grammatical way. In the following example: "what a wounded name,/ *Things standing thus unknown*, shall I leave behind me" (V, ii, 338–9, emphasis added), the absolute adverbial phrase is rendered by a conditional adverbial phrase. Schwob insists on keeping it: "quel nom mutilé, – *les choses demeurant ainsi inconnues* – vivra après moi" (p.168, emphasis added).[18] In this way, Schwob's French stays extremely close to Shakespeare's English syntax.

A fourth linguistic procedure which Schwob borrows from Shakespeare is ellipsis. Its use is very noticeable in the dialogues when the speakers shorten their expressions to achieve a quicker pace and more efficiency. In general the verb "to be" is omitted. Consider:

HAMLET.   What hour now?
HORATIO.   I think it lacks of twelve.
MARCELLUS.   No, it is struck.
                                    (I, iv, 3–4)

Schwob translates: "Quelle heure maintenant?" – "Je crois sur le coup de minuit." "Non, minuit sonné" (p.29). Schwob once again goes further than the English when he omits the verb "to be" from all three sentences.[19] Although in the main Schwob follows Shakespeare word for word, one finds in his translation italicized words which indicate a deliberate addition on his part. Sometimes these additions overcome ellipses in the English text which would block the comprehension or balance of the sentence if they were reproduced textually. Take this question and its answer, for instance, and Schwob's translation:

POLONIUS. What do you think of me?
KING.   As of a man faithful and honourable.
                                    (II, ii, 129–30)

POLONIUS. Que pensez-vous de moi?
LE ROI.   *Ce que je penserais* d'un homme loyal et honorable.
                                    (p.52)
[That which I would think of a faithful and honorable man.]

Although Schwob adds here to the English formulation, he nevertheless preserves the elliptic turn of phrase since, in order to write grammatically correct French he would need to write: "Je pense de vous ce que je penserais."[20]

As can be inferred from the above, Schwob and Morand go further than their predecessors in that they see no problem in stretching the linguistic codes of the receiving (French) culture to create a French prose style analogous to Elizabethan English in its use of archaic vocabulary and syntactic characteristics such as ellipsis, suppression of the article, and use of the adverbial adjective, not to mention the retention of Shakespearian doublets and epithets not common in French usage. Their translation does not respect the Cartesian notions of rational, clear, intelligible French. They do not aim for easy readability, but rather to evoke both Shakespeare's torrential vocabulary and the aural quality of his script. French hierarchical norms of syntax, bound to rational thinking and clarity, have been exploded by Schwob and Morand, whose love of words and imagery, sound and rhythm, reverberates throughout their translation, in the interests of breaking down what they see as the elitist barriers of French linguistic tolerance to embrace Shakespeare's more egalitarian conception of language.

While Schwob and Morand adhere to the linguistic norms active in the source text as closely as possible, it was not always possible for them to convey the multifaceted nature of Shakespeare's puns. For instance, the verb "to lie" (V, i, 109) meaning both "to be stretched in a horizontal position" and "not telling the truth," has been translated as "y être" and "ne pas y être" in the sense of "ne pas dire juste." Similarly, in the phrase "And many such-like as's of great charge" (V, ii, 43) the word-play on "as" and "as's" [asses] has been rendered by "en somme" and "bêtes de somme" [beasts of burden]. As can be inferred from these two examples, Schwob and Morand use strategies of compensation to suggest at least some of the allusions contained in Shakespeare's puns.

Very often the translators explain their choices and decisions in notes appended to the text. For example, since no plausible interpretation or correction for Hamlet's line "I know a hawk from a handsaw" (II, ii, 378) had yet been suggested, Schwob and Morand decided to translate the line by borrowing from François Villon's "Ballade du concours de Blois":

Mon amy est, qui me fait entendant
D'un cygne blanc que c'est un corbeau noir

[My friend taught me the difference
Between a white swan and a black raven]

and they translated the line in question as, "je connais bien un cygne d'un corbeau" (p.61) [I know a swan from a raven]. They recognize an obscene equivocation in Hamlet's teasing question to Ophelia: "Do you think I meant country matters?" (III, ii, 125), which they translated by its "absolute" meaning and in equivalence with a joke borrowed from the manuscript of a "rondeau" by the fifteenth-century poet Henri Baudé as: "pensez-vous que je le comprenais en rustaud?" (p.85). Hamlet's allusion to the "hobby horse" play (III, ii, 140–4) having become obsolete has been replaced by an allusion to the old fashion of "souliers à poulaine" (long pointed shoes), which were ridiculed in the sixteenth century, and by the refrain taken from Villon's *Ballade des dames du temps jadis*. The translation reads:

> Alors il y a espoir que la mémoire d'un grand homme puisse survivre à sa vie demi année, mais, par Notre Dame! il faut qu'il bâtisse des églises alors! ou bien il souffrira grande absence de souvenir avec les antiques *souliers à poulaine* dont l'épitaphe est:
> Mais où sont les *poulaines* d'antan.
>
> (p.86, emphasis added)

(Then there's hope a great
man's memory may outlive his life half a year. But by'r
Lady, 'a must build churches then, or else shall 'a suffer
Not thinking on, with the *hobby-horse*, whose epitaph
Is "For O, for O, the *hobby-horse* is forgot!")
(III, ii, 140–4, emphasis added)

The personification of the Spanish word "mallecho" (*malhecho*) in Hamlet's description of the dumb show as "miching mallecho" (III, ii, 148) has been represented by that of *Faux Semblant*, a character in the *Roman de la Rose* Schwob and Morand considered fitting here and who remained popular throughout the sixteenth century.

By dint of their allusions to late fifteenth-, sixteenth-, and early seventeenth-century French literature, especially to ballads, Schwob and Morand seem to go further than their stated goal of finding strategies of compensation for the English linguistic material. They seem to be attempting to reappropriate (at least in part) *La Tragique Histoire d'Hamlet* back into the native, oral tradition whence they believed it came. Although Schwob and Morand demonstrate a meticulous attention to detail in their translation of Shakespeare's vocabulary and turns of phrase in *Hamlet* by rendering them in virtually interlinear fashion, the way they are rendered in cribs, the translators attempt to reclaim *Hamlet* for the French oral tradition. The end result of their apparently scholarly attempt to translate Shakespeare "faithfully" is the acculturation (nationalization) of the *Hamlet* legend as part of the French *patrimoine* (patrimony). The contradictory nature of their efforts is to have at one and the same time expended much energy on a word-for-word rendition of the English source text, and to have inserted native French ballads to transform the English text into a text with perceived French parentage. Schwob and Morand's translation thus attempts to select and balance characteristics common to both source and receiving culture. They adhere to the linguistic and textual/narrative norms expressed in the source text, but when the allusions in that text are unclear they will substitute several lines with native textual material (Old French ballads and rondeaux, references to former French fashions and characters in popular French literature). In other words, Schwob and Morand introduced a cultural compromise between Old English language (they "historicize") and Old French literary forms (they "naturalize"). Their translation is a philological compromise between Old French and Shakespeare in an attempt to recreate, for French readers of their translation, the experience an English person has when reading Shakespeare. In this sense, the Schwob–Morand translation appears to be both of the "historicizing" and "naturalizing" type. Referring back to the "exoticizing versus naturalizing" axis as explained in the Introduction, Schwob and Morand chose to colonize the past, replacing Shakespeare's "exotic" allusions with native French ones. Although they "historicized" the linguistic and textual/narrative material of the source text, they decided to "naturalize" all space and culture-bound elements in Shakespeare's dramatic text, thus striking a blow for French literary imperialism.

Chapter 4
The blank verse shall halt for't
André Gide's *La Tragédie d'Hamlet*

Like Marcel Schwob, André Gide remained fascinated by Shakespeare throughout his life. In his collected *Journals*, which cover a period of sixty years, one can find myriad references to the playwright and his works, as well as to the difficulties presented by attempting to translate them. As a mature and respected French literary figure, Gide had published a translation of *Antony and Cleopatra* in 1921, yet the translation of *Hamlet* he had promised Georges Pitoëff in 1922 proved beyond his reach. As he said in the "Lettre-Préface" to his eventual 1946 edition of the play: "Ce premier acte m'avait fourbu; j'y avais consacré plus d'efforts qu'aux cinq actes d'*Antoine et Cléopâtre*"[1] [This first act wore me out! I put more effort into it alone than I did into all five acts of *Antony and Cleopatra*]. The Gide–Martin du Gard correspondence reveals that Gide forsook the work after many sleepless nights and long walks on the beach at Porquerolles "à la poursuite du mot juste ou de l'équivalence satisfaisante" [in search of the right word or a pleasing equivalent] had failed to inspire him to produce a translation he could proudly hail as an improvement over previous versions of the play.[2]

Gide's inability to translate *Hamlet* proved to be particularly galling for him, since he saw Shakespeare as the supreme incarnation of Romanticism, in the same way that he considered Racine to be the supreme classical playwright. A writer such as Gide, who remained throughout his life one of the most faithful and illustrious proselytes of Goethe's notion of *Weltliteratur*, a man who believed that the assimilation into the French canon of foreign literatures and ideas such as those of Shakespeare, Marlowe, Goethe, Novalis, Schopenhauer, Nietzsche, Poe,

Emerson, Whitman, and a host of others would generate ideas and new forms in his own writings, must have looked upon this failure to capture the essential Shakespeare "in good French" as a great personal defeat.[3] Gide laid the work aside and went on to other projects, but seven years later, in 1929, his single act of *Hamlet* was published in the December issue of the journal *Echanges*.

His *Journal* entries for 1890 and 1891 reveal that his passion for English and German literature had been a longstanding one. Twenty years before he learned English in 1909 he had read Walter Scott, as well as *Macbeth, As You Like It, A Winter's Tale, Coriolanus, Romeo and Juliet,* and *Antony and Cleopatra*, in French. Of course the intellectual climate of Paris at the turn of the century encouraged a cosmopolitan outlook, and other French literary figures such as Marcel Schwob, Paul Valéry, and Valery Larbaud were at that time contributing to the general sense of a common European *lingua franca* and to the *anglomanie* prevalent in the French capital.[4] In 1892 Gide went to Germany, where he saw a performance of *Richard III* in Munich (along with Lessing's *Nathan der Weise* and Schumann's *Manfred*).[5] In 1893, according to his diary, he went back to Shakespeare to read *Timon of Athens, King John, King Lear, Richard II,* and *Julius Caesar*. He also returned to Germany, further to acquaint himself with the philosophers and to hear performances of Wagner.[6] Back in Paris, Gide was mixing with the likes of Gosse, Rilke and Curtius, reacting against the French realist explosion by seeking out foreign works to which he could relate more directly.[7] He studied only those authors whose works struck a chord within him and which he thought would help him in his own literary creations to counteract the inward-looking tendencies of Naturalism, to reject what he saw as interminable journalistic depictions of family life among the French bourgeoisie and Zola's pseudo-investigative sensational exposés of the working classes. In terms similar to Schwob, Gide believed that Shakespeare, Goethe, and other writers would help him to enlarge the French perspective, encourage the French to look outside themselves again, and finally to come to terms with the defeat of 1870 that had caused so much painful soul-searching. The "Belle Epoque" in itself nurtured a pan-European outlook among the avant-garde; it became a sort of nineteenth-century Renaissance where universality opposed the narrow nationalism and patriotism of 1870. Therefore Gide's preliminary norm in attempting to translate *Hamlet* for the first time was to stimulate new movements within French literature: using a translation to enrich the receiving French culture. Only with the help of outside influences did Gide think French literature could be great again.[8]

The desire to enrich French works of art with other European ideas, and the "transplantation" of these ideas into his own work as a way of generating new ideas and of exploring what constituted the real André Gide, were the reasons underlying his initial attempt to translate *Hamlet*. Gide may have abandoned the play, but the thinking which prompted him to try to translate it in the first place would cause him to complete the task in similarly depressed circumstances in the 1940s.

The project was revived when, quite by accident, he met Jean-Louis Barrault in Marseille, in the war-torn France of 1942. Gide was suffering from depression at the time, and was fleeing the war and his own unhappiness to stay in Tunisia. His chance encounter with Barrault proved to be a meeting of two likeminded souls.[9] The mood of France was not unlike that in the period following the Franco–Prussian war; in 1942 the French had become once more a saddened and introspective people. Both men saw in *Hamlet* something which could break them out of their depression and enable them to propose new beginnings. As Barrault put it in his *Nouvelles Réflexions sur le théâtre*:

> When we become weary from searching for the rare we turn to Shakespeare to make us feel like living once more, to revive our hearts and to make us focus on humanity ... Shakespeare is in vogue at the moment. He is one of us. In fact Shakespeare also lived in times of murder, revolution, and catastrophe, like us ... between two ages, where faith has been lost but still not regained during a period of doubt, like us.[10]

Both Gide and Barrault saw the echoes of the times in *Hamlet*: revolution and death, turmoil and confusion, but both also recognized the importance of the character of Fortinbras, since the idea that peace and the forces of good would ultimately prevail was, at that time, uppermost in their minds.

Barrault had admired Gide's translation of the first act of *Hamlet*, since in his opinion it demonstrated a deep respect for the text, and for Shakespeare's innate rhythm and profound sense of realism, unlike Guy de Pourtalès' 1923 translation of the play, which he had performed earlier in 1942 at the Comédie Française. Barrault thought Pourtalès' translation had overemphasized *Hamlet*'s romantic qualities, so in Marseille he urged Gide to help him to convey to the French public "the truthful, realistic tone of Shakespearian poetry."[11] Barrault published two meditations on the work of Shakespeare that bear witness to his painstaking consideration of the character of Hamlet, whom he saw as not only an actor in the play but a symbol of all Shakespearian tragedy and a figure of great significance for modern times. Barrault saw Hamlet as an "existential" character who finds himself torn between doubt and faith, but lucid enough to translate this dilemma into an overall questioning of the validity of individual action, and even of existence itself in a rotten, corrupt world. In his opinion Hamlet is a character who, after overcoming the temptation to kill himself, pulls himself together and offers himself as a sacrifice to enable the creation of a new world order where faith will once again be possible. In wartime, Barrault knew that a new translation of *Hamlet* that reflected these ideas would have profound allegorical significance, and it was in these terms that he encouraged Gide to help translate "the truth" beneath the surface of Shakespeare, so that the French people and French literature could be reborn, and so that new ideas, new beginnings, a belief in the future and in peace as the result of chaos could be encouraged.

So it was that Gide felt himself drawn back to his original project: he realized that to give an undertaking to produce such a translation could offer him consolation both in the desperate general circumstances and in so far as his return to *Hamlet* would perhaps fulfill its original purpose of infusing his own poetics with new ideas. With Barrault's encouragement, he plunged into the task with vigor. He worked for three months, from six to eight hours daily, on the translation which, he hoped, would see him through his own literary crisis: "perhaps soon I will find it in myself to undertake more personal projects."[12] This rapid completion of *Hamlet* proved to be exactly the therapy Gide had claimed it would be in the 1890s.[13] In completing his translation of *Hamlet*, he somehow found the inspiration necessary to overcome his troubles and to write the personal, soul-searching *Thésée*, which appeared in 1946.

Barrault, too, was well pleased with the result. He saw Gide's diligent version of the play as one which perfectly conveyed those ideas he considered most relevant to any performance of Shakespeare:

> It is all about finding the solution to this problem of mechanics, repairing the clock by adjusting the wheel – a matter (in theatre) of settling all accounts, of cleansing humankind of its passions, of restoring it to health and life all the stronger for the experience: about giving back truth and justice. That is the real task of the dramatist, and the basic social function of theatre.[14]

Having abandoned his first translation of *Hamlet* because, in his words, "in order to write good French, one has to get too far away from Shakespeare," Gide considered his wartime *Hamlet* to be greatly superior to all earlier *Hamlet* translations in that he had created it specifically for Barrault's stage and actors.[15] Gide's *Hamlet* was first published in 1945, in New York, with the English original on facing pages. A year later the translation stood alone in a Paris edition of the text, which became the version used by the Compagnie Madeleine Renaud/Jean-Louis Barrault for their inaugural performance at the Théâtre Marigny, in Paris, on October 17, 1946, complete with a musical score by Arthur Honnegger and sets by André Masson. It was Barrault's first performance since leaving the Comédie Française.

Barrault may have praised the translation, and Gide may have publicly stated that he thought it an improvement on all previous *Hamlet* translations which, in his view, sacrificed rhythm, lyrical power, cadence and beauty to mere exactitude, but he still felt the need to introduce his version with a "Lettre-Préface" outlining the difficulties he had faced.

From this "Lettre-Préface," it is possible to deduce the translational norms Gide set up when he began his task. Among these norms, a certain hierarchy seems to establish itself: firstly and most importantly he strives for clarity, both in meaning and syntax. In order to establish clarity, Gide naturalizes the source text, making Shakespeare's allusions and turns of phrase French. By gallicizing the text in this way Gide sought to make it immediately relevant to a modern audience. His reasoning was that, if Barrault's production was to convey a message of hope for the post-war years, then the audience should be left to focus on that message and not become caught up in a web of obscure philological signification. Hence the second of Gide's translational norms: he sought to produce a translation in "good" modern French, not the archaized French of Schwob or the classical French of so many of his predecessors. Gide's third concern was for Barrault: he had conversed long enough with the latter to know that he was above all concerned with the symbolic nature of the play in time of war, and thus paid great attention to the preservation of the vital rhythm of the original in his modern French prose. Most of all, with Barrault in mind, the translation would have to be playable in French. The three translation criteria – clarity, modernity, and rhythm – go hand in hand, but clarity remained Gide's overriding concern in producing a new translation of *Hamlet* for the twentieth century.

In the "Lettre-Préface," Gide characterizes the text of *Hamlet* as one which expresses often simple sentiments in the most complicated of possible manners: a text which represents the very height of artifice, or more probably of art, and far surpasses Corneille's most nonsensical declamations in its tendency to plunge the reader into a poetic trance far removed from reality. The English text, in his opinion, has a tendency to bathe everything in so special an atmosphere that even the most fanciful flights of speech strike one as being natural. The difficulty for the translator is that of transposing this supranatural reality into a much less malleable language, a language constrained by strict grammatical and syntactic requirements, that is to say a language as precise and prosaic and, in Gide's mind, as anti-poetic as French.[16] Yves Bonnefoy recognized the same qualities in Shakespeare's original but, as is revealed in the following chapter, he worked in the tradition of Mallarmé to attempt to produce a French translation of *Hamlet* that would have the same supranatural poetic qualities as Shakespeare's original.

Because he believed that the French language was basically anti-poetic, Gide chose to write his version in prose, a clear modern French version of a play he saw fit to purge of most of its baroque elements, precisely because he was of the opinion that it was impossible to render them in good, grammatical French. The compromise he made in order to finish his translation of the play was that, instead of just staying as close as possible to the linguistic and textual norms of the original in the manner of François-Victor Hugo, Schwob, Pourtalès, and Jacques Copeau, he sought to write a "playable" version of the text for Barrault's company, a version which sounded French and which flowed effortlessly in order to be as understandable as possible to a French theatre audience that did not have the time to meditate on all the implications of Shakespeare's language when caught up in the complexities of his plot. Gide's ultimate aim was to "explain" Shakespeare as clearly as possible for the benefit of the audience of theatre goers and in this, he claimed, his translation would differ from the French *Hamlets* mentioned above. Otherwise, he would never have reapplied himself to the task. His reasoning was that in terms of "accuracy," of staying close to the multiple codes of the original dramatic text, he could not hope to go beyond Hugo or Schwob, and therefore he would attempt to produce a playable, "breathable" text that would flow in a way quite distinct from "normal" translations, which he thought tended to be stilted.[17] He would have to resort to multiple rewordings and rereadings to make this possible.

Gide hoped to produce this "intelligible" translation of *Hamlet* by giving accuracy of content preference over accuracy of form, producing a prose translation instead of a verse translation. Bonnefoy would later fulminate against Gide's decision when he argued that separating form from content makes one lose all sense of the original. Perhaps Gide anticipated future criticism along these lines when he translated Hamlet's comments on the actors' impending arrival in II, ii, 324–5, "the lady shall say her mind freely, or the blank verse shall halt for't," as "nous accorderons à la jeune première toute liberté d'expression afin d'éviter les vers faux" (p.105) [we shall allow the leading lady complete freedom of expression to avoid any lines that fall flat].[18]

Whereas Schwob followed the source text word for word, Gide felt free to cut and add to the original's number of words. He followed a rationalist tendency to clarify the original (thereby making it more easily playable and memorable for both actors and spectators), cutting whenever Shakespeare uses "redundant" word clusters (although not repetitions which he kept for reasons of rhythm and oratorical force) and adding words whenever he believed the original image to be somewhat elusive to the French reader/spectator. Jean-Claude Noël has him adding and deleting three times as many words as Schwob in his attempt to translate *Hamlet* for the modern French theatre. Noël goes on to state that Gide appropriates all the deletions made by Schwob in his translation, as well as one of his additions.[19] Indeed, in his haste to finish the task, it appears that Gide borrowed more than a little from the translations of his predecessors. In so doing, Gide places his text firmly within the long tradition of French Shakespeare translations, but with the aim of clarifying and modernizing them for a new generation of readers and spectators. In his "Lettre-Préface," Gide announces that certain of his predecessors had made his task much easier, since their efforts cannot be faulted for accuracy; this allowed him to use previous French *Hamlets* as a starting point and to concentrate on making his own version clear, modern, and playable.

Most of Gide's own deletions concern Shakespeare's doublets or pleonastic expressions which are virtually inadmissible in French. In the interests of clarity, he invariably drops one of the two nouns which make up a Shakespearian doublet. Doublets and tautological expressions that come across as redundant in French are most often dropped, or sometimes clusters of Shakespearian nouns are simply exchanged for French verbs. For instance, Hamlet asks Horatio what he is doing back from Wittenberg (I, ii, 169–73):

> HORATIO. A truant disposition, good my lord.
> HAMLET. I would not hear your enemy say so,
> Nor shall you do my ear that violence,
> To make it truster of your own report
> Against yourself

is translated by Gide as:

> HORATIO. On vagabonde, mon bon Seigneur.
> HAMLET. Je ne permettrais pas à votre ennemi de le dire, et vous violentez mon oreille en vous calomniant ainsi.
>
> (p.37)

> [HORATIO. I'm playing truant, my good lord.
> HAMLET. I would not allow your enemy to say so, and you are offending my ear in maligning yourself so.]

At the end of Scene ii of the first act Hamlet urges Horatio, Marcellus, and Bernardo: "Let it be tenable in your silence still" (line 248) which is rendered by Gide succinctly as "n'ébruitez rien encore de ceci" (p.43) [don't spread this about any more]. The tendency to cut down Shakespeare's doublets and noun phrases and replace them by a single verb is found throughout Gide's translation, in an attempt to make the original more harmonious to the French ear.

Whenever Gide does rearrange or delete parts of the original dramatic text, he explains the reason for his intervention in endnotes. He apologizes, for instance, for having shortened and simplified the "rugged Pyrrhus" speech which Hamlet starts and which the First Player picks up and finishes in II, ii, 466ff. He is not sure whether this speech is a satire on Nashe or Marlowe or whether it is a quotation from a slightly older play of which Shakespeare might be the author in collaboration with Marlowe, as some critics have suggested (p.115). Most critics agree that this speech is Shakespeare's. But Gide cannot decide whether Shakespeare approves of it and gives it as an example or whether he ridicules it. At any rate, he considers the intention too subtle for it to be captured by any translation. And, since the tone and appearance of these verses is more important than their meaning, Gide elected to simplify them at the cost of their exact signification. Indeed, he shortened and simplified all the speeches of the travelling players in *Hamlet* (pp.113–15).

Elsewhere Gide departs somewhat from the English to render a passage more accessible. Instead of just translating "Norway" as "Norvège," he clarifies the French, using "le roi de Norvège." Whenever a literal French translation strikes him as too obscure, Gide makes the referents of the original passage explicit. He is particularly conscientious in introducing the characters to the audience and in clarifying their family relationships. "Young Fortinbras," for instance, is spelled out as "le fils de Fortinbras" – the two Fortinbrases of Norway and the two Hamlets of Denmark are clearly distinguished for the French spectator. Characters as well as places and situations are presented by Gide in as detailed a fashion as possible, to make their signification immediately apparent to the French. When Hamlet asks Rosencrantz and Guildenstern how they have been, Guildenstern answers: "On Fortune's cap we are not the very button" (II, ii, 229), which Gide domesticates as: "Sur le chapeau de la Fortune nous ne sommes pas *la cocarde*" (p.99, emphasis added) [the rosette]. When describing the French horseman Lamord, who hails from Normandy, Claudius uses the expression "A very riband in the cap of youth" (IV, vii, 73) which Gide naturalizes as "Simple ruban au *béret* de jeunesse" (p.225, emphasis added) [on the beret of youth]. More striking, however, are some allusions to French authors. In the Hecuba monologue (II, ii, 565) Hamlet refers to himself as a "John-a-dreams" which Gide, indirectly alluding to Laforgue, renders as "Pierrot lunaire" (p.119). (Laforgue did, indeed, write his own parody of *Hamlet*, entitled "Hamlet ou les suites de la piété filiale.") Another allusion to a French writer, this time an epigonal one, occurs in Hamlet's advice to the players (III, ii). Hamlet does not want any of the visiting actors "to split the ears of the groundlings" (line 10) or have one of them "o'er-doing Termagant" which "out-herods Herod" (III, ii, 13–14). In Gide's translation we find that the actor should not "[rompre] les oreilles du parterre" [deafen those in the stalls] and should avoid "de pareils sur-Artabans" (p.137) [outdoing Artaban]. Artaban was one of the heroes of the seventeenth-century French novelist and playwright la Calprenède, who was appropriated into the French language as a metaphor of pride and "préciosité." Gide made such changes in an attempt not only to have the play strike a chord with the French audience, but to have it play smoothly. For the play to read well "in good French," he would occasionally have to gallicize whatever struck him as too exclusively Anglo-Saxon. One of the objections he made to Schwob's text was that it strayed too far from French linguistic norms and conventions: he criticized Schwob's tendency to imitate Old French phraseology even on the level of word order and grammar.[20]

The second of Gide's stated translational norms was to produce a modern translation. This he attempts to do by choosing not to transpose elements of Shakespeare's original where he sees the English as too baroque, convoluted, or obscure to be translated into modern French.

Where Gide does use modern vocabulary and/or allusions, it is often with the intention of preserving his overall objective – clarity – and of making the text flow so that the audience can focus on the acting. For example, he translates "this distracted globe" (I, v, 97) (alluding to Hamlet's head as well as to the Globe Theatre and its audience), as "ce monde affolé" (p.67) [this crazy world]. As a modernizer, Gide thought it unnecessary either to keep the word "globe" (as Schwob and others had done), or to refer to its larger meaning – the Globe Theatre – in a footnote. His desire was to make the text meaningful in wartime France, not to uncover the multiple significations of Shakespeare's text in a philological manner, as Schwob's "archaizing" translation had done. For Barrault's sake, Gide wanted to endow his translation with the power to draw an allegorical connection between the death of the old (Danish) order and the new (Norwegian) dawn at the end of Act V, and the post-war renaissance of France. In other words, his translation would look forward rather than backward, as he considered Schwob's had done. In his opinion, his own translation of the line "ce monde affolé" suited his purpose much more than the alternatives furnished by his predecessors in that it did not detract from the message Barrault would be trying to act out on stage: the audience would grasp straightaway that the "crazy world" in question was that of 1940s Europe, not Elizabethan England.

Since the translator in question is André Gide, modernity turns out, however, to be a rather elusive norm. As something of a classical writer himself, and one heavily influenced by Goethe at that, Gide tended to write *Hamlet* in his own style, with a double result: both the rebirth of the text in French and the rebirth of Gide in the text.

Although Gide has made an obvious attempt to render the play in the (at times) familiar tone of the source text, his classical leanings are such that he eventually adopts a more elevated, "tragic" vocabulary than the original. By and large he manages to conform to twentieth-century usage, but his very erudition prompts the retention of certain archaisms such as "male" (bad), "féal" (loyal), "comparoir" (to compare), and "guerroyer" (to wage war). As opposed to Schwob, who preferred to translate in concrete terms, Gide sometimes has recourse to abstract expressions. Where Schwob has "vieillard" [old man], Gide prefers the more allegorical "la sénilité" [senility]; instead of Schwob's "des coups de pieds" [kicks], Gide writes of "les rebuffades de l'indigne" [the rebuffs of the unworthy].[21] He tends to adopt a more classical, unified tone than Shakespeare; his French is mostly learned and stripped of baroque metaphor. Boldness in the English is diluted to suit French taste. Hamlet's words, "I will speak daggers to her, but use none" (III, ii, 403), are translated as: "Je ne percerai son coeur qu'en paroles" (p.161) [I will pierce her heart, but only with words]. Similarly, when Hamlet warns his soul not to act on his words in III, ii, 405, "To give them seals never, my soul, consent!" Gide has him speak less metonymically: "Celle-ci (mon âme) n'acquiescera jamais aux menaces de mes paroles" (p.161) [My soul will never assent to the threats of my words]. It would be remiss to suggest, however, that Gide shies away from translating Shakespeare's colloquial or down-to-earth expressions. In III, iv, 93–5 he translates Hamlet's conversation with Gertrude, "Nay, but to live/ In the rank sweat of an enseamèd bed,/ Stew'd in corruption, honeying and making love/ Over the nasty sty," as: "Quoi! Vivre dans le suint ranci d'une couche crasseuse, infuser dans la pourriture, et, sur un fumier puant faire l'amour" (p.175) [What, to live in the rancid grease of a filthy bed, stewing in rot and making love on a stinking dung heap].[22]

While he wished to produce a clear, modern translation of *Hamlet*, Gide was very careful not to sacrifice those poetic qualities of Shakespeare's text Barrault thought endowed it with hope. Playability was a prime consideration in his translation strategy. Furthermore, in his "Lettre-Préface," Gide states that he considers the translator who renders only "the meaning of the text" to have accomplished "almost nothing."[23] His aim was to ensure the playability of the text by preserving the sense of poetry without the form, keeping the rhythm, the élan, and the vitality of the original intact, but intelligible.

Gide does not use an iambic pentameter, of course, since English versification differs fundamentally from French prosody, yet he nevertheless made sure of capturing some suggestion of Shakespeare's rhythm, which was of great importance to Barrault. Noël highlights Gide's version of Gertrude's speech telling of Ophelia's death (IV, vii, 171ff.) as containing a surprising deviation from normal French grammatical usage in order to convey shock: "la branche où elle prenait appui s'est brisée, lasse de ses trophées herbeux et la laissant choir elle même parmi les larmes de la rivière" (p.231) [the branch on which she was leaning broke, tired of her weedy trophies and letting her fall among the tears of the river]. For Noël there is a surprising concurrence of the adjective "lasse" and the present participle "laissant," which betrays Gide's normally smooth French in favor of a sense of Shakespeare's (in this passage) a-cadenced, measured, almost mechanical rhythm.[24]

Throughout his translation, it appears that Gide wishes above all to focus on the exterior aspect of a word, arranging his sentences carefully to create a rhythmic effect. He listens to a word, appreciates its sound quality in English, and then chooses an equally cadenced expression in French. This is precisely where Gide's translation, in the opinion of many commentators, goes one step beyond previous versions of *Hamlet*. Its rhythmical qualities ensure that the text plays well, that each sentence is well balanced, well constructed, and well rounded. In this, Gide lived up to his desire to produce a stage-worthy text. Yet where the French text gains a rhythmical quality often undeveloped in previous translations, the necessary alterations have resulted in shifts in other areas.

By highlighting clarity, modernity, and rhythm as his watchwords, Gide chose to unravel in places Shakespeare's tight fabric of words and images, and consequently much of Shakespeare's animal imagery, for example, is downplayed. As already pointed out by other critics, Polonius' counsel with his daughter makes him denounce Hamlet's advances as "springes to catch woodcocks" (I, iii, 114) which Gide translated, like Schwob, as "Miroir à alouettes" (p.51) [decoy, which suggests skylarks]. Polonius' remark later echoes in Laertes' line when the latter realizes he has been trapped: "as a woodcock to mine own springe" (V, ii, 300). This becomes "comme un gibier pris à mon propre piège" (p.275) [like game caught in my own trap] in Gide's version, no longer reflecting the father/son relationship in the same animalistic terms. Similarly, Hamlet no longer insults his mother by alluding to Claudius who will call her "his mouse" (III, iv, 184). Gide has Claudius call her "son petit rat" (p.181) which puts her on the same footing as Polonius and obliterates the more general allusion to the "Mousetrap" the actors will set for the king and queen.[25]

Another interpretative shift in Gide's translation occurs when he vents his anticlerical sentiments. The queen's description of Ophelia's flowery appearance (IV, vii, 165ff.) mentions "long purples,/ That liberal shepherds give a grosser name" (IV, vii, 169–70) which Gide readily translates as "ces digitales pourprées auxquelles nos bergers libertins donnent un vilain nom" (p.231) [these foxgloves which our libertine shepherds give a rude name]. The result is that Gide provokes a deliberate *contresens*: in the opinion of most critics these shepherds are not "modern" (atheistic) freethinkers, but free-speakers in the sense that they neglect to watch their tongue.

Given the fact that French and English prosody are based on two exclusive systems, Gide's avowed goal of bringing out Shakespeare's "poetry" before a typical French audience was an ambitious one indeed. Most critics have agreed that Gide was largely successful in his endeavors, because he paid attention to the rhythm and tone of the original. In Hamlet's monologue, for instance, at the end of the second scene of Act II the exclamation, "O! what a rogue and peasant slave am I!" (II, ii, 547), is turned into the rhetorical repetition, "Oh! quel rustre je suis! quel esclave informe!" (p.119), and Hamlet's final goodnight to his mother (III, iv) in which he refers to Polonius' corpse:

> Indeed this counsellor
> Is now most still, most secret, and most grave,
> Who was in life a foolish prating knave
> (III, iv, 214–16)

is elaborated upon by Gide in a rhetorical tripartite construction:

> Parbleu, ce Conseiller de Cour, si loquace, si niais et si vain durant sa vie, le voici maintenant bien discret, bien réservé, bien grave!
>
> (p.183)

[Indeed, this Counselor, so loquacious, idiotic and vain during his life, is now most still, most discreet, most reserved, and most grave.]

The translation of this passage represents a clear example of Gide's adherence to the rhythmic balance of the source text.

To a great extent, Gide's *Hamlet* has managed to satisfy both literalists and theatre directors alike. It manages to avoid many of the problems which face a literal translator by being flexible and open to compromise.[26]

Barrault was most gratified by the end result. Together with Gide he analyzed the translation word for word, and together they sought to create the right atmosphere for the subsequent representation of the play. In her account of the Paris production, Nancy Lee Cairns stresses that Barrault sought to recreate the atmosphere "of the twilight hour," the "entre chien et loup" when "life itself seems to hesitate, and the mood, that of ambiguity, the period of passage from life to death."[27] It was a very dark, somber production, where a black-clad Hamlet stood against neutral-colored curtains, and all the other characters seemed "to bathe in a greyness which allows the attention of the audience to remain entirely on the psychological development."[28] Yet at the end of the spectacle, Fortinbras entered in a costume of "scarlet and black and white with a tremendous plumed helmet; his soldiers resplendent in chequered doublets and long hose," the very culmination of Gide's and Barrault's 1942 discussions in Marseille.[29]

Barrault's knowledge of what was needed to leave an impression on the French audience and Gide's ability to provide him with a text which would strike a chord with that audience undoubtedly popularized the play in France. The fact that Barrault virtually commissioned Gide to complete the translation in the first place suggests that he was seeking to move toward a true "théâtre du peuple" with his conception of Justice in the person of Fortinbras:

> A tragedy cannot simply end with the death of its hero. It must expose *the complete, general and total solution* to human conflict. A play is a play and not just a role; a tragedy ends thanks to the dispenser of justice, not only thanks to the victim.[30]

Chapter 5

Yves Bonnefoy's *La Tragédie d'Hamlet*
An allegorical translation

"Monseigneur Hamlet est un prince, hors de ta sphère,/ C'est impossible, impossible!" (p.66) [Lord Hamlet is a prince – out of thy sphere, it's impossible, impossible].[1] This is what Polonius tells the king he said to Ophelia (Shakespeare's II, ii, 141) in Yves Bonnefoy's translation of *Hamlet*, but the lines could equally well apply to the task of translating the play into French, at least in the opinion of this poet/translator, who has so far produced four retranslations of his original *Hamlet* (1957), the latest being a 1988 revision performed under the populist direction of Patrice Chéreau at Avignon and later in Nanterre.[2]

Yet Bonnefoy remains a believer – he is firmly persuaded of the ultimate translatability of *Hamlet*; indeed his four reworkings of the play attest to his ability to see through Polonius' allegorical trickery. In quasi-baroque allegorical fashion, refusing to rely on appearance alone (since he is aware of Polonius' use of irony to break down the face-value of language), Bonnefoy's translations of *Hamlet* attempt to answer the play's call for a liberation of the work of art from its own linguistic entanglements.[3] They go beyond empirical significance to evoke the imagery of Bonnefoy's own poetic output, where each and every word is accorded the power to speak of far more than itself. Bonnefoy's translations, like his own poetry, rely on a world of allegorical interplay to suggest a cosmic presence.

As a translator and literary critic, Bonnefoy is guided by his own poetics. One of the major poets to come to prominence in France since the end of the Second World War, and probably the major French lyric poet of this period, Bonnefoy's is a metaphysical poetry of modern times. Its clear, depersonalized voice gives aesthetic form to questions of presence and absence, time and place, being and nothingness.[4] Such themes are familiar to the literary public as part of the general post-war existentialist scene, yet as an existentialist poet Bonnefoy is not so much influenced by his contemporaries as by the past. He is a mystic "in reverse" who situates a divine presence without God in the objects of this world. Influenced by Baudelaire, by the Gnostics and Hegel, by the allusive imagery and density of the Symbolists, and the imagination and vision of the Surrealists, one finds in his poetic universe the ghostly but very real presence of Rubens and Giotto, Bernini and perhaps especially Shakespeare, with whom he has been obsessed since the 1950s and to whom he has returned time and again to translate *Hamlet, Julius Caesar, King Lear, Macbeth,* and many other plays.[5]

Bonnefoy's various translations of *Hamlet* (published in 1957, 1959, 1962, 1978, and 1988) contain extensive endnotes. He takes care to mention his source texts as being the John Dover Wilson (1934/6) and Harold Jenkins (1982) editions of *Hamlet*, and to explain any difficulties he encountered when translating the original. It is notable that Bonnefoy's revisions contain fewer endnotes as he becomes more comfortable with the text, having found it possible to integrate whatever explanations contained therein in the text itself. There were ninety-two endnotes in the 1962 edition, compared to sixty-four in the 1988 edition, and the latter are generally shorter. The notes themselves consist of textual, interpretative explanations of lines, metaphors, individual words, and puns Bonnefoy found difficult to render into French. For example, Hamlet's retort to the king in the second scene of the play, "A little more than kin, and less than kind" (I, ii, 65), is translated by Bonnefoy as "Un peu moins qu'un neveu, mais rien moins qu'un fils" (1962, p.26) [a little less than a nephew, but no less than a son], with a note containing the original. His later attempt at the same line: "Bien plus fils ou neveu que je ne le veux" (1988, p.23) [much more a son or nephew than I would wish], both incorporates Shakespeare's wordplay ("kin" is one letter less than "kind"; "neveu" is a telescoped version of "ne-le-veux"), and echoes Jean-Michel Déprats' solution: "Un peu plus que neveu, moins fils que tu ne le veux" [A little more than a nephew, but less of a son than you would wish].[6]

Sometimes the endnotes explain the shifts Bonnefoy made in

order to interpret certain lines, and they frequently indicate where he follows and where he deviates from clarifications made by Jenkins or Dover Wilson. His most radical shift from those English editions occurs in the first scene, where he assigns to Marcellus a line generally attributed to Horatio: "Alors, a-t-on revu la chose cette nuit?" (p.15) ("What, has this thing appeared again tonight?") (I, i, 21). Bonnefoy's decision to attribute the line to Marcellus is explained in his first note: it is based on his belief that Horatio appears incredulous and only half-interested in spending his time waiting for the Ghost.

Allusions such as those by Dover Wilson and Jenkins in their notes to other texts by Shakespeare's contemporaries and the Ancients are no longer present in Bonnefoy's latest version. Rather, he devotes his attention to explaining his translation decisions, usually in places where he has attempted to retain the ambiguity of the English line. In comparison to the 1962 version, many translated lines have become shorter and tighter, and often aim at creating an effect derived from Bonnefoy's reading of Shakespeare's dramatic text. Horatio's line in the first scene, which explains the warlike attire of the Ghost – "A mote it is to trouble the mind's eye" (I, i, 112) – was translated in 1962 as "Oh, ce n'est là pour l'oeil de la pensée/ Qu'une poussière irritante!" (p.21) [it is but a speck of dust in the mind's eye], and in 1988 as "Encore ces poussières/ Pour irriter l'oeil de notre pensée!" (p.19) [more dust to irritate the mind's eye]. Not only do the later version's words have less of a heroic (Racinian, or acculturated) ring to them but the alliterations and assonances reverberate with greater force. The meter of the 1988 version follows the rhythm of the original more closely than the earlier version, and hints at the possibility of a French qualitative/syllabic pentameter.

The basic problem with translating *Hamlet* into French, according to Bonnefoy, is that French and English are metaphysically different, so much so that any diligent translator, instead of merely expecting the classical alexandrine to capture Shakespeare's poetic style, or seeking to avoid the problem of transposing Shakespeare's innate rhythm by adopting a prose style, must attempt to formulate some kind of system which will mediate this basic linguistic (and philosophical) difference.

Not unlike Walter Benjamin, Bonnefoy conceives of the task of the translator as one revolving around language itself and not, as some would have it, as an exercise centered exclusively on content and meaning.[7] The translator's ultimate aim should be to hint at pre-Babelian, Edenic speech – a "pure" form of language more exalted than either the language of the original or the target language, which necessarily remains unsuited to its content, overpowering and alien. The linguistic and philosophical norms of French constitute an implicit partial critique of Shakespeare; inversely, the linguistic and philosophical norms of English contain an implicit partial critique of all French-language translations of Shakespeare. As Bonnefoy sees it, his task is not that of translating *Hamlet* for its own sake (otherwise he would not have felt compelled to return so often to the text), but that of ensuring its after-life, not so much in the French-speaking world as in the realm of what Benjamin terms "pure, or divine language" itself.

By downplaying those ideational elements in his own language which are ripe with Platonic qualities, with "essences," and by choosing to amplify that which transcends its own natural condition, Bonnefoy hopes to produce in it "the echo of the original."[8] Therefore, as he conceives of it, the true goal of the translator is the denaturalization of natural language. In short, Bonnefoy sees his task as nothing less than that of converging the French and English languages, re-establishing a community between two distinct codes based on a common ancestry in a higher spiritual order where all meaning ultimately ceases to exist.

In the postface to the Mercure de France edition of his 1962 translation of *Hamlet,* Bonnefoy published an essay, "Shakespeare et le poète français," in which he underlines the fact that the French language has yielded no definitive version of the play to compare with the German Schlegel and Tieck translation which has been a mainstay of the German repertory since the early nineteenth century.[9] Instead, each previous translation of Shakespeare into French has tended to be a reflection on one or other of the myriad questions thrown into relief by the English, that best happened to fit contemporary literary preoccupations. The Ducis translation, in the best classical traditions, revolved around the conflict of love with duty, whereas the Dumas translation highlighted the melodramatic side of Shakespeare in a break with the preceding classical interpretation. In short, according to Bonnefoy, there has been no all-encompassing version of any Shakespeare play in French: no single period in French literary history has been able to render the substance of a *Hamlet* or a *King Lear* in language befitting the original. And even though Supervielle, Leyris, and Thomas have produced admirable versions of individual plays, in Bonnefoy's eyes they have failed to impose a single, authoritative voice on their edition of the *Oeuvres complètes* (1954).[10]

The reason why so many French translators have tried and failed to capture the spirit of Shakespeare in their own language is largely historical. The problem is clear to Bonnefoy: none of Shakespeare's French contemporaries offered a translation of his work.[11] The late sixteenth or early seventeenth centuries would have been the ideal time for the French to produce translations in the style of Shakespeare, before the advent of the Académie Française in 1629 and the classical strictures imposed by the "Judgement of the Academy on *The Cid*" (1638) – an historical and linguistic context exploited, as will be noted in the next chapter, by Michel Vittoz in his 1977 translation of *Hamlet*. As Bonnefoy sees it, classicism bogged down subsequent attempts to translate Shakespeare, owing to the restrictions imposed on French tragedic style by the dodecasyllabic classical alexandrine and the relatively limited vocabulary judged to be fitting for the representation of tragedy. Voltaire's version of the famous "To be or not to be" soliloquy illustrates just to what extent the influence of the Académie distorted French translations of *Hamlet*. It begins thus: "Demeure, il faut choisir, et passer à l'instant/ De la vie à la mort, et de l'être au néant" [Stay, the choice must be made, and journey without remiss from life to death, from being into the abyss].[12] Given this example, one can appreciate Bonnefoy's distaste for Ducis' subsequent translation, in which the latter's use of alexandrines, the three unities, and his modifications of Shakespeare's narrative structure, which puts Hamlet in the situation of having to choose honor and glory over love (by making Ophelia Claudius' daughter), highlight the impossibility of producing a "faithful" rendition of Shakespeare under the classical system.

The Shakespeare translations produced from the Revolution to the end of the Second Empire, although freed from classical rules of prosody, tend to be haunted by melancholy, Romantic heroes and suffer from a lack of immediacy and presence by attempting total literalness at the expense of poetry. Whereas Shakespeare's Falstaff seems to be real, to step out of the page and speak to us directly, Bonnefoy remarks that François-Victor Hugo's prose translation of *Henry IV, Part I* represents Falstaff as "distant, attenuated, toned down, as (if seen) through a windowpane."[13] French Romantic translations reveal themselves to be mere shadows of the original – the words no longer have the poetic power to reflect the English version's immediacy and vitality. In Bonnefoy's words, "c'est un Shakespeare décorporé" [they are Shakespeare disembodied], and this in spite of the Romantics' attempt to avoid the pitfalls of becoming entangled in the web of classical verse forms by falling back on prose.[14] Yet there lies the problem: once one translates Shakespeare into prose, one risks losing the larger-than-life quality of the characters, which in English is also proof of their status as living, breathing, immediate incarnations; in other words, one forfeits the vital quality of the original blank verse.

In Bonnefoy's opinion, even previous twentieth-century translators of Shakespeare have not managed to overcome this problem. Although they were free to choose whichever form of verse or prose translation they thought would solve past difficulties, they nevertheless failed to render the characters real, continuing to have them talk as if from behind a plate-glass window. Gide's translation, in particular, is subjected to heavy criticism by Bonnefoy. In his opinion, Gide's *Hamlet* lacks the ability to convey the real. Bonnefoy dismisses it as "un théâtre de marionnettes, littéraire, faux et affecté" [puppet theatre: literary, false and affected].[15] From the above one can infer that Bonnefoy has studied the French translation tradition with regard to Shakespeare's work, that he not only places himself within that tradition but challenges it, especially in the form of his immediate predecessor, Gide.

By underlining what is lacking in previous French *Hamlet* translations, Bonnefoy highlights the basic characteristics of his own (translation) poetics: his concern with immediacy and presence, vitality and incarnation, his search for a place to come face to face with the "other," the real. Yet Bonnefoy, again not unlike Benjamin who refers but glancingly to the historical relationships between languages in his essay "The Task of the Translator," soon leaves this domain, the better to focus on the linguistic thrust of his allegorical exposé.

In Bonnefoy's eyes, so many inadequate translations cannot have been produced by accident: his explanation for all of the previous failures targets a basic defect in the French language itself, which tends to reduce the English language to an idiom that seeks to confine any notion of the real, of the universal, into neatly formulated intelligible essences. In other words, whenever it is faced with translating poetry, French is doomed to render that poetry only in its own very specific "essential" terms. The French language has its own inescapable poetics. Therefore, any translator seeking to transform Shakespearian English into a faithful French equivalent will have to overcome the fact that the two languages are metaphysically different and thus very difficult to equate.[16] Because of its dual nature (although Bonnefoy does not mention this explicitly, one can define its roots as Anglo-Saxon and Anglo-Norman), English has the ability to resonate on a real, specific level, as well as on a timeless, universal level. To the French, Shakespeare's poetry appears as a "brave new world" without restrictions or limitations of any kind, focusing on universal but very real problems, whereas Racine's poetry is the force which sustains a closed, hierarchical world driven by its own laws and its own essential force.[17] A Racinian play is limited to clearly delineated situations and sentiments cleansed of reality in that nothing is allowed to stand in the way of honor and duty, not even love. The outcome is known once the exposition has outlined the problem in question, and all that stands between the opening act and the death or ruin of all concerned is the flow of brilliantly executed alexandrines. The action is swift, inevitable and uncomplicated, driven by a language composed of what Bonnefoy calls "essences intelligibles."[18]

A Shakespeare translator's main task should therefore not be that of gallicizing the Anglo-Saxon but that of breaking down the very restrictive nature of the French language. Bonnefoy recognizes that all French poetry is not Racine, of course, but his explanation of the nature of French demonstrates why a language owing so much to Racine, his contemporaries, and their conception of "essences" cannot capture the vitality and presence of Shakespeare's poetry. According to Bonnefoy, the general law of French poetry is that of exclusivity, whereas

English, and Shakespeare in particular, is inclusive. The English language is defined allegorically by Bonnefoy in terms of "ouverture" (or "openness"), as a language rich in words and tones whose nature he compares to a mirror. French, on the other hand, is defined in terms of "fermeture" (or "closure"), as a language which designates something only to exclude anything else which is not designated: its general nature is that of a closed world, of a sphere.[19] To return to the opening quotation, Bonnefoy sees in it his own predicament – that of a French writer seeking to translate Shakespeare from within the "sphere" of the French language:

> Et à la jeune personne, voici comment j'ai parlé:
> "Monseigneur Hamlet est un prince, hors de ta sphère,
> C'est impossible, impossible!"
>
> (p.66)

(And my young mistress thus I did bespeak:
"Lord Hamlet is a prince, out of thy star.
This must not be.")

(II, ii, 141)

Trapped within the sphere of a Platonic idiom, the translator must seek a way to capture the real, Aristotelian nature of English: he or she must transform the "sphere" into a "mirror" capable of reflecting the nature of the original. Previous French translations failed because they were essentially compromises which accepted the *status quo*: they saw no way of breaking out of the sphere, resigning themselves to the fact that French was a Platonic idiom which could not be forced into an Aristotelian direction.[20] Bonnefoy totally rejects this notion, insisting that the translation of English into French should not be a transposition from Aristotelian patterns of signification to Platonic "equivalents." Any true translation owes it to itself to be not merely faithful to the content, but to be a metaphysical reflection, a mediation of the way of thinking of a particular language – an attempt to render the original material faithfully in terms of poetry and tone. Consequently, in order for it to transpose Shakespeare into French with any degree of fidelity, the French language must be pushed to Aristotelian limits of signification in so far as that is possible. For Bonnefoy, therefore, translation becomes an interrogation of itself, a language's fight with itself.[21] His hope is that his attempts to translate *Hamlet* will prove successful in that he sees scope for communication between Shakespeare's combination of realism and metaphysicality and modern (post-Mallarméan) French poetry, which is itself characterized by an "idéalisme renversé" [inverse idealism].[22] In other words, Bonnefoy not only gives a pseudo-deconstructive reading of French *Hamlet* translations but also sees himself as a French poet resisting an idealist and essentialist French poetics in the wake of Mallarmé.

The French language must be wrenched free of its idealistic, conceptual nature; it must be guided beyond classical forms and the closed nature of its prosody to become a language able to evoke the universal and the real. The translator of Shakespeare must strive to preserve the meter and tone of the Bard without constricting them, thereby stretching the limits of French poetry, creating "une poésie qui se cherche" [a self-reflective poetry].[23] The translation process should begin at the precise point where the two languages confront each other – becoming a battle for precedence between two forms of thought. By means of the necessary transformation French poetics will undergo in the process, Bonnefoy hopes that by translating Shakespeare he will propel the French language toward a new spiritual level.[24] In this essay Bonnefoy reveals his poetics of translation to be a code-changing activity. As a translator he will resist the process of acculturation in an effort to retain as much of the foreign source culture as possible. In a dialectic exchange the linguistic (and philosophical) systems of English and French will confront one another, and expose each other's nature, thereby creating a new "spiritual" system.

In translating Shakespeare, Bonnefoy has shown himself to be acutely aware of the quiddity of his own language: the fact that French nouns are burdened with a grammatical gender and the fact that French adjectives are forced to agree with the nouns they qualify.[25] It is virtually impossible to continue to refer to the Ghost in French as "it," not only because of that language's predilection for *le mot juste* (*la chose* conveys neither referent, reality, nor presence in French), but also because French, when referring to an unspecified shape, uses the personal pronoun *il*, which immediately personifies and endows the "thing" with a gender. As a result of a dialectic exchange, the English system here informs the French: Bonnefoy has tried to avoid the ensuing confusion by using "c'est." Not only are French nouns marked by gender; as in English they can be marked for plural. Shakespeare's plural nouns are, however, often transformed into singular nouns. In his 1988 translation Bonnefoy tends to use one singular noun in preference to the more general plurals he used in earlier versions. Compare the following:

Sans quoi nous sommes des reflets sinon des bêtes
(1962, p.156)
[Without which we are reflections if not beasts]

Sans quoi on n'est qu'une ombre ou une bête
(1988, p.143)
[Without which one is but a shadow or a beast]

with Shakespeare's line:

Without the which we are pictures or mere beasts
(IV, v, 87)

This is the case even when one would least expect it, for instance in Hamlet's soliloquy (I, iv, 23): "Et dans *l'homme* il en va de même" (p.39) ("So oft it chances in particular *men*") (emphasis added). This tendency to delete is reflected in Bonnefoy's own poetry, where he often attempts to evoke the "presence" of a word by using singular nouns (of course this process also serves to confirm the abstract, Platonic nature of the French language). The tendency to delete does not stop there. In his 1988 version of *Hamlet*, Bonnefoy has also deleted some of the present participles which he used in previous editions to link two lines together, following his criticism of their excessive use in T. S. Eliot's *The Waste Land*.[26]

Furthermore, Bonnefoy will often choose nouns instead of adjectives: for instance, the Ghost warns Hamlet in the fifth scene of the first act that his story may cause his "knotted and combinèd locks to part" (I, v, 18) which Bonnefoy translates as "et déferait tes boucles et tes tresses" (p.43) [and would undo your curls and tresses].

Like his previous versions, the 1988 edition of *Hamlet* often shows Bonnefoy deleting Shakespeare's use of doublets which come across as "bizarre" in French. Leroy C. Breunig quotes Mallarmé as having referred to them as "une mode de rhetorique singulière" [a singular form of rhetoric], giving examples such as "head and chief," "mirth and jollity," "the motive and cue for passion."[27] Bonnefoy eliminates doublets throughout: two similar verbs become one, two similar nouns are reduced to one and sometimes two different adjectives are reduced to one, both for reasons of economy and as a way of suggesting the "presence" he believes permeates Shakespeare's text: "how express and admirable, in [his] action" (II, ii, 305)[28] becomes "comme il est résolu dans ses actes" (p.74) [how determined he is in his actions]; "within the book and volume of my brain" (I, v, 103) becomes "Dans le livre de mon cerveau" (p.46) [in the book of my brain]; "The pales and forts of reason" (I, iv, 28) becomes "les tours de sa raison" (p.39) [the towers/trickery of their reason]; "To hear and see the matter" (III, i, 21) becomes "assister au spectacle" (p.88) [to attend the show]. As it reduces the number of words contained in the source text, Bonnefoy's translation spins an increasingly tight web of allegorical interrelationships between those words it chooses to retain. Each word in the translation necessarily evokes other meanings implicit in the source text. Bonnefoy also added punctuation marks where the original has none, and, in a manner typical of the allegorist, he indicates emblematic nouns and highlights symbolism by freely capitalizing certain other nouns. For example, he capitalizes "Ciel" [heaven] and "Etat" [state] throughout the play, but especially in the first and last acts.

In a second postfaced essay to his 1962 *Hamlet* translation, "Transposer ou traduire *Hamlet*," Bonnefoy addresses the specific question of how to push the French language to the Aristotelian limits to which he referred.[29] He does this in reaction to a proposal by Christian Pons (in the issue of *Etudes Anglaises* entitled "Shakespeare en France") that the best way to render the duality of meaning, the concrete and the intangible nature of Shakespeare's language, is to translate it into flexible Claudelian "versets," even if the likely result is a translation which turns out to be longer than the original.[30] Since, as Bonnefoy has suggested, French excludes all it does not designate, Pons in turn suggests that one needs to develop explicitly all that which is implicit in Shakespeare in order to capture his use of image faithfully. Pons had criticized Bonnefoy for having "inadequately" translated Marcellus' line from the opening scene of the play – "Therefore I have entreated him along/ With us to watch the minutes of this night" (I, i, 27), suggesting that the meaning contained in this line needs to be developed as follows: "Afin qu'il surveille avec nous les ténèbres, et ce lent écoulement des heures, tous les moments de la nuit l'un après l'autre" [In order that he may keep watch with us over the darkness, and this slow passage of hours, every single moment of the night one after the other][31] and not so succinctly as Bonnefoy's "Pour épier ces heures de nuit" (p.15) [To watch over these nocturnal hours].

Bonnefoy recognizes that English, and especially Shakespeare's English, is a language rich in ambiguities, and that to choose between possible interpretations of a line is a thankless task. He stresses the importance of the allegorical thrust of Shakespeare's work, the idea that, in Benjamin's words: "Every person, every thing, every relation can signify any other."[32] Objects cannot retain their own identity; they are in perpetual danger of being summoned to appear in allegorical reference to something else.

As a translator, Bonnefoy is very consistent in his use of a word once he has decided it is the correct solution to a problem: if he decides on the word "rêve," to render "fantasy," for instance, he will continue to do so throughout.[33] Moreover, he is extremely conscious of Shakespeare's use of repetition (as opposed to his decision not to transpose Shakespeare's doublets), and will try to make that internal rhythm come across in French. Hamlet's monologue in I, ii has the following example: "O, that this *too too* sullied flesh would melt" (I, ii, 129); Bonnefoy has this: "O, *souillures, souillures* de la chair! Si elle pouvait fondre" (p.26, emphasis added).

In keeping with his comprehension of Shakespeare's multireferentiality, and the fact that Bonnefoy tries to infuse his own poetics and translation practice with imagery at once allegorical and concrete, his *Hamlet* translates the very bestiary of Shakespeare's cosmos. In her article, "Woodcock et bécasse: avatars d'une métaphore shakespearienne," Germaine Marc'hadour reviews in chronological order the various French translations of Polonius' line to Ophelia and Laertes' to Osric which, in their identical use of imagery and rhetoric, link the first and last acts of *Hamlet*, as well as linking father and son.[34] When Ophelia reports to her father that Prince Hamlet "hath given countenance to his speech, my lord, with almost all the holy vows of heaven," Polonius answers: "Ay, springes to catch woodcocks" (I, iii, 113). Similarly, after Hamlet and Laertes have wounded one another with the poison-tipped rapier, Osric asks: "How is't, Laertes?" and the latter answers: "Why, as a woodcock to mine own springe, Osric/ I am justly killed with mine own treachery" (V, ii, 300–1).

Shakespeare twice uses the words "woodcock" and "springe" together. Whichever French expressions are chosen to translate them, Marc'hadour insists that the translator should repeat in the last act the words of the first act, since Laertes, son of Polonius, has no doubt borrowed this metaphor from his father.³⁵ He appears to echo his father, a man full of "words, words, words," fond of proverbs and "similitudes."³⁶ She argues that in *Hamlet* everyone sets bird-traps to catch the other, and that the hunter often becomes the quarry. Marc'hadour believes that retaining the bird image is the best way to express this idea. Further analyzing bird imagery in *Hamlet* as it relates to her interpretation of the play, she concludes that a writer's choice of metaphor constitutes his or her idiosyncratic palette or interior universe. Whoever suppresses one instance of animal metaphor in the work of Shakespeare upsets his whole "ménagerie." If a cliché such as "not a mouse stirring" in the first scene is meant to adumbrate the frenetic "Mousetrap" of the third act, and if this mousetrap incorporates Polonius the "rat," and, one may add, Gertrude "the mouse," then one should not, according to Marc'hadour, neglect any element of this bestiary.³⁷ She quotes Bonnefoy's first translation:

POLONIUS. Ah, piège pour les bécasses!
LAERTES. Ah, Osric, je me suis pris à mon propre piège comme une bécasse.³⁸
[POLONIUS. Ah, a trap to catch woodcock!
LAERTES. Ah, Osric, I'm caught in my own trap like a woodcock.]

which is preserved intact in all his subsequent versions. Bonnefoy's decision to preserve Shakespeare's bestiary in his translation not only highlights his sensitivity to the rhythm and metaphor of the original dramatic text; it also manages to satisfy the most demanding of critics, in the shape of Marc'hadour. As a translator, however, Bonnefoy's main aim is not that of pleasing the normative critic. His translation decisions are prompted by his own understanding of Shakespeare and his own poetics.

Thus he rejects Pons' solution to the problem of transposing Shakespeare's "meaning" as being nothing short of treasonable, since his overelaboration leads to a rupture of the poetic tension of the original.[39] Pons' is also too easy a solution, and in the best tradition of the modern French poet, Bonnefoy declares that in order to translate at all well, one must first set oneself the most impossible of tasks: one must struggle with two distinct systems of thought and let this confrontation produce the translation. By explicitly stating "meaning" Pons also cancels out the most intimate feature of Shakespeare's theatrical language – its duality; the opposition between the conscious and the unconscious levels of poetry uncovered by the play.[40] The problem with Pons' extrapolated translation solution, according to Bonnefoy, is this: when pronounced onstage, Marcellus' plea for Horatio to stay with him "to watch the minutes of this night" may just project all the meaning Pons' longer version spells out to the audience. Yet it is probable that Shakespeare did not intend Marcellus to grasp the full significance of his words. All meaning, in Bonnefoy's eyes, does not need to be spelled out onstage. To develop unto apparent exhaustion what is but one possible aspect of meaning is to abandon any other more mysterious meaning, and as such it is not the philosophy which best captures the spirit of the Elizabethan age. In fact, eventually this course of action will diametrically oppose the translator to Shakespeare's thought. Bonnefoy quotes Hamlet's line, "The time is out of joint. O, cursèd spite,/ That ever I was born to set it right!" (I, v, 188), noting that never was there anything so pessimistic, so far removed from the security of a faith, as *Hamlet*.[41] Here, in a link with Benjamin's analysis of the baroque *Trauerspiel*, or tragic drama, Bonnefoy sees the prince as the paradigm of melancholy; the only purpose underlying his actions is the maintenance of an order which is destined to collapse. The genius and madness of Hamlet the allegorist remain forever impervious to the practical application or meaning of the word: revealingly, the very ideas with which Pons is preoccupied. An intuition of impending doom and disaster haunts the Elizabethan conscience, and Hamlet's torment, his search for and failure to find a viable order underpinning the work he inhabits, are precisely that which, according to Bonnefoy, Shakespeare's blank verse expresses to such perfection.

In terms of characterization, there has been a shift in the attitude of male figures toward the female figures in the 1988 edition. When Claudius refers to Gertrude in the second scene, for instance, he said in the 1962 version: "Nous l'avons prise pour femme" (p.25) [Taken to wife] and in the 1988 version: "Nous l'avons ... épousée" (p.22) [wedded] ("Taken to wife" (I, ii, 14)). Whereas the queen said in 1962: "Non par la faute du roi!" (p.159) [It's not the king's fault] to convince Laertes of Claudius' innocence regarding Polonius' death, she now says much less respectfully: "Non par sa faute à lui!" (p.146) [It is not his fault] ("But not by him") (IV, v, 130). Both Ophelia's and the queen's lines have become more straightforward, for instance in the third scene of the first act, where Ophelia answers her father. The 1962 version has "il m'a poursuivie de son amour" (p.41) [he chased me], and the 1988 version "il me presse de son amour" (p.37) [he forces it on me] ("My lord, he hath importuned me with love" (I, iii, 110)). Bonnefoy completely rewrote Ophelia's songs in IV, v; whereas he translated them in *rime riche* in the 1962 version, the 1988 version accords them more complexity in their largely alternating rhyme schemes. The queen's lines in this scene (before she sees the now crazed Ophelia) have been rendered less ambiguous; her aside, according to Dover Wilson, "accounts for the Queen's reluctance to see Ophelia and gives us the only glimpse of her real state of mind after Hamlet's departure to England."[42] Shakespeare's

> To my sick soul, as sin's true nature is,
> Each toy seems prologue to some great amiss.
> So full of artless jealousy is guilt
> It spills itself in fearing to be spilt
> (IV, v, 17–20)

is initially rendered by Bonnefoy in abstract, dense, almost neoclassical terms (1962):

> A mon âme malade, et c'est la loi du péché,
> Le moindre rien semble l'annonce de grands troubles.
> Le crime est si inquiet, et si gauchement,
> Qu'il fait de son effroi l'artisan de sa perte.
> (p.153)

[To my sick soul, and such is the law of sin,
The smallest thing seems to portend great turmoil.
Crime is so clumsily restless
That it makes its fear the workhorse of its loss.]

By 1988, however, his translation has become much more evocative and straightforward:

A mon âme malade, et c'est cela le péché,
Un rien semble l'annonce de grands malheurs.
On est si anxieux, quand on se sent coupable,
Si démuni, qu'on meurt de craindre la mort.
(p.141)

[To my sick soul, and that is the sin,
A trifle seems to portend great misfortune.
One is so anxious, when one feels guilty,
So destitute, that one dies from fear of dying.]

The king's lines, too, have become tighter and sometimes, as in his prayer, more spiritual, reflecting an interior world behind his statements. These various language-specific and character-based shifts all serve to fit the overall tendency of the 1988 edition, which is toward leanness and stress on the more "Aristotelian" aspects of the play. Indeed in his quest for an allegorical style by which to evoke reality and presence, Bonnefoy often makes the French lines shorter than those of the original; paradoxically, his tendency toward the deletion of "redundancies" sometimes results in an essential, almost Racinian economy of expression. Horatio's line, "A countenance more in sorrow than in anger" (I, ii, 232), becomes "Plutôt triste qu'en colère" (p.31) [more sad than angry]. Racinian economy of expression perhaps, but anything which smacks of Racinian bathos or heroism in the monologues of the 1962 version has been deleted by 1988. Hamlet's monologue at the end of III, ii is affected as follows: 1962: "Si cinglantes soient mes paroles, ô mon âme" (p.123) [However bitter my words may be, oh, my soul]; 1988: "Mon âme! Aussi cinglantes soient mes paroles" (p.113) [My soul! As bitter as my words may be] ("How in my words somever she be shent/ To give them seals, never my soul, consent!" (III, ii, 404–5)). The heroic "sur ma vie" [on my life] of 1962 has become "j'en jurerais" (p.155) [I'd swear to it] ("Upon my life" (IV, 7, 91)).

For Bonnefoy, as for Benjamin, translation does not revolve primarily around meaning. It does not recognize sense as the mediating force between living language and living revelation.[43] His interest lies with language beyond its utilitarian and symbolic functions, beyond the burden of extra-linguistic meaning and the structures on which it rests. His concern is not with the realization of intention but with the affirmation of a reality for which all allegorical interpretation must necessarily be a conduit. Words are but witness to the advent of a form – they cannot hope to capture and retain meaning, since meaning is essentially an abstract idea.

The form should in no way be subordinate to the content. One absolutely cannot ignore the pentameter in *Hamlet*, and the power it has to express Shakespeare's thought at once specifically and metaphysically. For Bonnefoy, when translating Shakespeare it is imperative to preserve the poetic tension created by his verse form. It may have seemed initially that the verset offered any prospective translator of Shakespeare a flexible means by which to render a complex work, since it uses both long and short lines, and comprises both poetry and prose, as does Shakespeare's verse, but because of the way it is used by Claudel, and the underlying notion it conveys of "souffle" standing for both poetic and religious inspiration, it conveys a naive and dogmatic view of the world, which one does not find in Shakespeare. Claudel's "flexible" form unfortunately projects a missionary's zeal to sow optimism and contentment wherever it is applied. Whereas, on the surface, it appears to be the one French form capable of reflecting Shakespeare's world order and versification, on further examination the verset is rejected by Bonnefoy as an insufficiently ethical or spiritual solution to the problems posed by *Hamlet*.[44]

The problem for any translator of *Hamlet* is to find a poetic form which does not break down the whole structure of the original. The verset is a bold solution: it attempts to cut a swathe through French and English prosody and confront the diversity of the original. Yet in Bonnefoy's opinion, the use of versets establishes a counterfeit order on the relaxed nature of the English form, creating a false poetic rhythm which attempts to make sense of the multiple questions thrown up by the elaboration of the original. It imposes its own order where there is none in Shakespeare's dramatic text. *Hamlet* is a work which relies on chaos and unanswered questions – "To be or not to be?" – and Bonnefoy suggests that one no more has the right to translate *Hamlet* in versets (imposing clarity and order in the manner of Racine where there is none in Shakespeare) than one has the right to substitute an answer for that which wishes to remain a question.[45] Hamlet's monologues bear witness to his endless effort to seek meaning in his predicament: he inhabits a world where nothing is sure or fixed, in much the same way as Bonnefoy, the translator, constantly searches for a sense of the real in his revised versions of the play. In Bonnefoy's eyes translators must not impose a false meaning, they must only "transpose" in turn this feeling of the unknown. They need to translate the idea that the scope of the questions raised by the work is greater than the sum total of possible answers to them. Yet, at the same time, translators must not just render an image by its incomprehensible reflection, nor must they submit to the opaque or the plain meaningless under the banner of fidelity to the text.[46]

Blind parallelism is just as dangerous as substitution of answers for questions, since one thereby loses the interior significance of a line at the expense of the exterior meaning.[47] Yet with Shakespeare, an interlinear, word-for-word translation is sometimes the only approach to take, the only intelligible solution of an enigma irreducible to its meaning. With Shakespeare, it is impossible to stick to principles or all-encompassing formulas for translation. The only principle to which Bonnefoy has been able to adhere with any conviction is that of a dialectics in the Greek sense of reciprocal enlightenment, of a dialogue in which the inevitable transpositions should concern the most minute detail possible.[48] He does not proclaim literalness, but a degree of attention to detail which, in his opinion, ensures the poetic importance of his enterprise. In other words, Bonnefoy largely conceives of translation in dialectic and even allegorical terms, along the lines of Benjamin's definition of allegory: "allegory ... means something different from what it is. It means precisely the nonexistence of what it presents."[49]

Bonnefoy uses allegory as the principal means by which he can bring his poetic language into closer contact with the dialectical reality of being.[50] Not only does he try to internalize death in his own poetry; in his translation of *Hamlet* he also allegorizes the presence of loss: the presence of an original Shakespeare play written in a particular English verse form which will necessarily disappear in any translation. Although averse to quick and easy solutions, Bonnefoy makes it clear in this essay that the choice of a comparable French form in which to translate Shakespeare's verse is uppermost in his mind.

Any translator who embarks upon a text must, consciously or unconsciously, make certain fundamental choices as to the overall structure and form of the finished product. In his essay "Comment traduire Shakespeare" (1964), Bonnefoy argues, at least in the beginning, that all approaches to translation are justifiable and can reveal themselves worthwhile on condition that the text to be translated fits the approach chosen by the translator.[51] When faced with translating a play such as *Hamlet*, certain decisions need to be made from the outset, and the most fundamental of these decisions relate to form. Firstly, should one translate in verse or in prose? If the answer is verse, then should the verse be regular?

According to Bonnefoy, no one in France initially claimed that translating Shakespeare in verse was a bad thing, as far as fidelity to the original was concerned. Equally, those who translated in prose, such as Schwob and Gide, thought they lost nothing of the poetic power of the English. They must have assumed that at least part of the poetic substance of the original – images, symbolism, and metaphor – was preserved in their versions of the play, in the apparent belief that the content of a play can to some extent be separated from its form. The success of these prose versions bears witness to the fact that verse is only one device among many to express in a more striking, more majestic, and more memorable way that which remains essentially a description of a state of consciousness, or of an aspect of the human condition.[52] Nevertheless, Bonnefoy asks, is this in essence what Shakespeare would have wanted? Is prose a viable means of translating Shakespeare? If we distinguish Shakespeare from the philosopher, also an analyst of the human condition, is it not because within his verse there lies this dual ability to state the real and the ideal, the concrete and the intangible? Take Hamlet, for example.

He cannot easily be explained unless we recognize that he is a metaphor for the whole writing process whereby Shakespeare proceeds to create *Othello, King Lear, Macbeth,* and *Henry VIII.*[53] *Hamlet* cannot be understood or translated separately from the rest of Shakespeare. Therefore any translation must encompass events larger and more portentous than the obvious ones played out onstage. The presence on Shakespeare's stage of not just Hamlet and the events taking place at Elsinore but also echoes of *Julius Caesar, Richard II,* and *Henry V* must be made to ring forth by means of a form grander than mere prose descriptions of events onstage. Bonnefoy insists that in Shakespeare real drama and real tension come about just as much as a result of Hamlet's relationship with his Shakespearian predecessors as of his relationships with Gertrude and Claudius.

Poetry, much more than prose, has the capability to evoke the unseen, sacred order behind Shakespeare's work. Poetry alone can illustrate the plight of a Hamlet confronted by doubt, weighed down by the collective angst of his predecessors. Indeed it is the notion of the unseen that "literal" translations (for example Gide's) fail to capture, according to Bonnefoy. Equally, since Shakespeare is theatre, and represents only a part of the Elizabethan theatrical canon, the translator must not only situate Hamlet in relation to other theatrical heroes; he or she must also be aware of the spatial requirements of Elizabethan stage practice, of the idea of presence versus emptiness, evoked by the text.[54] A literal prose translation will neglect this spatial dimension and consequently an entire layer of meaning suggested by the play. The choice between a verse and a prose translation thus becomes for Bonnefoy not only a technical decision but one which affects the whole outcome of the experiment. If a verse translation using Claudel's versets tends to answer the great questions raised by the work with religious optimism, and imposes its own sense of order on Shakespearian chaos, then prose translations such as Gide's attempt to translate *Hamlet* address these same questions too rationally, preferring to focus on the obvious. They are too conceptual and analytical, ignoring that which is not explicit in the text, and which makes up so much of the overall effect of the original. Bonnefoy's own poetry reflects a poetics of absence: he celebrates the empty space, traces, fragments, the unstated intemporal quality of a language whose syntax speaks mysteriously of presence. This is a quality he suggests should be present in any translation of Shakespeare, but how best to render it? He has accepted that verse is preferable to prose, but French verse translations of Shakespeare have typically been composed of alexandrines evocative of that very tightly significant, essential world he is trying to avoid.[55]

In refusing to use versets and rejecting a prose translation, Bonnefoy's main concern is to turn outward, toward the world, instead of seeking consolation by imposing some supreme conceptual order onto a poetry he cannot contain. Translation will be a struggle which will see the translator strive to make his or her own tongue communicate with outside reality. This cannot be done by falling back on the classical alexandrine. Partisans of this verse form had argued that regular prosody was the form of expression Shakespeare himself used and was therefore the one form capable of recreating all the aspects of his work. Such a form, not having specifically been invented by the author, but used by him to create his own work of art, presents itself as a link between individuality and a common spiritual order.[56] It evokes the possibility of a belief which could be shared by everyone. The very problem with the use of regular verse, however, is that it implicitly accepts the idea of an orthodoxy, necessarily standing for a supreme myth, or of order which would seek to regulate and classify Shakespeare's meaning. According to Bonnefoy, "the pentameter limps" because humankind can no longer trust in a myth, or escape doubt or confusion. Thus it happens that the word truly denies the form, the real refutes the idea.[57]

For Bonnefoy, translating Shakespeare in regular verse would make a travesty of the tension between the ideal and the real inherent in the original. Regular verse would bestow upon the text an impression of artifice which the forced ingenuity of the translator could only aggravate: the characters would adopt excessively conventional tones of voice which would come across as bizarre affectation to anyone familiar with English. Graham Dunstan Martin has illustrated how the Chevalier de Châtelain's nineteenth-century translation of *Hamlet*, in alexandrines, tends to a symmetrical neatness of expression which perfectly illustrates Bonnefoy's point:

> La mort, pays lointain, qui se perd dans les brumes
> De la pensée humaine, et dans ses amertumes,
> Pays inexploré dont jamais voyageur
> N'est encor revenu, jette le froid au coeur.
>
> (Death, that far-off country lost in the mists
> Of human thought, and in its bitterness,
> That unexplored country from which never has a traveller
> Returned, chills the heart.)[58]

The choice of such a regular, pre-established form, in Bonnefoy's eyes, limits the scope of the translator to solve the problems posed by the text of the original.

Bonnefoy proposes that the solution lies in the use of free verse. Free verse offers many advantages to the translator, since it can be a form which enhances poetic intensity without imposing too rigid a framework on the text to be translated. With respect to Shakespeare's prosody, whose regularity has a meaning, free verse is perhaps the best way to echo that meaning, at least if one succeeds in imposing an average length of meter upon that verse as a guideline. Due to the constant echo of lines of a certain length, Bonnefoy manages to reflect Shakespeare's regularity; that he refuses to adhere to a closed metric structure is indicative of his concern to remain open to the imperfection and unpredictability of the real. Bonnefoy's "regular" line is one of eleven syllables – the first half promising the regularity of an alexandrine, the second half refusing it. The first six syllables promise an evocation of the ideal, classical world, but the next five seem to finish before their time, thus stopping short of the ideal, still within the realm of the real. The caesura in Bonnefoy's line, coming as it does after the sixth syllable, does not lead to a complete separation of what it divides; as an instance of critical power it only prevents the different parts and levels of the line from mixing freely while simultaneously keeping them together and apart.[59] Gallicizing Shakespeare's line by using a twelve-syllable alexandrine would negate its difference, deforming the truth of this "other," whereas the hendecasyllable ensures that the presence of that which is the other preserves its fundamental independence. A line of eleven syllables illustrates in part the openness of a French self (Bonnefoy) to an English "other" (Shakespeare): two elements which, although retaining their individuality and difference, are nevertheless able to share the one possession they have in common – the word, a force that is defined by Bonnefoy as being at the very root of our origin, and by Benjamin as pure language.[60] Translators thereby have the option, by choosing free verse, of using alexandrines as and when they see fit, for example to render spiritual intensity when the need arises. Indeed throughout his translation Bonnefoy exercises his option to be flexible, often even more flexible than the original. He varies his solutions to the problem posed by the French alexandrine, which causes him at times to start out a verse with four syllables, for instance in Laertes' line when he reacts to seeing Ophelia enter with flowers in her hands: "Burn out the sense and virtue of mine eye!" (IV, v, 157). Bonnefoy translates in 1962: "Consumez le pouvoir et la vie de mes yeux!" [Consume the power and life of my eyes!] (p.161), and in 1988: "Brûlez mes yeux, faites-en de la cendre!" (p.147) [Burn my eyes, turn them into ashes!].

This flexibility of meter allows him to impose what he considers to be an English rhythm onto the French language. Most of the changes he made since the 1962 version relate to capturing the sound and the rhythm of Shakespeare's dramatic text as well as a more direct, concrete, and active rendition of its "meaning." To obtain this effect, he expands and contracts the syllable count, at times getting close to *vers libre*, now and then lapsing into prose, but at all times one has this feeling of order imposed by the regular reappearance of the hendecasyllable.

Of course the use of the hendecasyllable seems too neat a solution to Bonnefoy's problems. It does not address a difficulty which free verse attenuates but does not obliterate: the fact that in the work to be translated all invention has already been done for him, and whatever his freedom to maneuver in the undefined space created by free verse, he recognizes that a form only has real poetic value when it puts the translator at risk. Like Shakespeare, whom he perceives as living through his plays, as proceeding from *Hamlet* to *Lear* to *Henry VIII*, Bonnefoy feels the need to take risks: to live and relive his poetry through his several revisions of the text of *Hamlet*. Therefore, if poetry is to be translated at all, the translation will, according to Bonnefoy, have to be subject to his own poetic risk-taking. He will have to live the translation, as Shakespeare did the original, and come up with his own approach. Hence the use of his own free verse. Given this, how can he hope to be faithful to Shakespeare at the same time?

Bonnefoy has forced himself into the position of questioning the validity of translating Shakespeare at all, and even the translator's right to do so. He looks at Shakespeare's world as a very personal creation, and the development of Shakespeare's poetic skills over the course of several plays as evidence of the maturation of Shakespeare as an individual. Having considered all this at great length, Bonnefoy finds solace in the fact that Shakespeare's poetry has another life. Once this poetry takes on theatrical form, although still profoundly personal, it has the ability to strike a chord within the collective consciousness of all spectators. Since *Hamlet* is also a spoken word available to all, Bonnefoy feels free to understand and recreate it poetically on his own terms. He considers himself at liberty to translate those elements he sees as being part of our collective consciousness, thereby reconstituting the spatial architecture of the original, translating only certain elements and leaving space where space existed, in order that the profound, secret Shakespeare still has the space to establish himself in the gaps left by his text.[61] The general tendencies of Bonnefoy's translation remain: an attempt to make the French language accommodate the realism of Shakespeare's style, a preference for the concrete (if possible) as opposed to the previous conceptual French-language renditions of the play, a deletion of Shakespearian doublets and tautologies, an approximation of comparable sound effects by means of alliterations, assonances, internal rhyme, and metrical effects, an avoidance of the French alexandrine, a displacement of normal stress and a basic pattern of the hendecasyllabic line. The tautness of his 1988 French version is supported by such devices as "concrete imagery (or just words instead of images), pithy syntax, terseness of expression, exclamatory repetitions and forceful combinations of sounds."[62] Bonnefoy attempts to translate many a Shakespearian image literally, as concretely as possible, and to make his French as graphic as the spirit of the play allows. Nevertheless, he does not always transpose the theatrical imagery in Shakespeare, such as the "ear" metaphors or the many "play" allusions in the characters' lines. Furthermore, as Monique Nemer points out, he does not always respect the spatial rhetoric of the play, which comes across to her as strange in the work of a poet so concerned with "presence" and "absence" in language.

In her article, "Traduire l'espace," Nemer underlines that few translators in the dramatic realm have concerned themselves with the reading (and thus the translation), not of specific spoken words, but of space.[63] There is nothing metaphorical in her use of this term – it is not a reference to the "elsewhere" (cities or islands) where Shakespeare situated his tragedies and comedies. The hidden spatial rhetoric in Shakespeare's language was a theatrical requirement. Shakespeare's writing was produced by and for a particular and concrete space: that of the Elizabethan stage. If one agrees that in dramaturgical matters, meaning is not enclosed only in linguistic operations, one can ask oneself how – and to what extent – the translation of a play conceived for the Elizabethan stage space can be influenced and informed by the mental representations of a translator working more or less consciously with an Italian stage model. Nemer considers some translations of *Hamlet* to measure the consequences of this equivocation. The way in which the Elizabethan stage is divided into upper, inner, and forestage is implicit in Shakespeare's writing: there are no stage directions for example. It is this interweaving, according to Nemer, of seeing and saying, of representing and naming required to conform to Elizabethan stage practice that most translations, trapped in a one-dimensional system, overlook and cause to disappear.[64] One could even ask oneself whether one of its consequences is not the tendency to psychologize Shakespeare's text: failure to offer a symbolic reading of the space leads one to take only the verbal exchanges into account. According to Nemer, from this inadequacy in the source stage-space and the target stage-space equation, a certain number of incongruities result.

Nemer notes that stage space as it existed for Shakespeare allowed for a dramatic type of writing which could be qualified as a writing of juxtaposition. She notices, however, that although the text of the First Folio juxtaposes without comment the scene "in the plain" (IV, iv) to the scene in the interior (IV, v), the text edited by Dover Wilson, which Bonnefoy translates, introduces as a stage direction "some weeks pass" – as if time is responsible for distending the elliptic contiguity of the two scenes. If it is a characteristic of theatre to inscribe its rhetoric in space, it also has the characteristic of inscribing space in its rhetoric. Nemer wonders whether the poetic imagination of Shakespeare is not in part structured by spatial representations which themselves render a vision of the world in metaphorical terms. The notions of "high" and "low" are alternately invested with political, ethical, and dramatic significations. Nemer even suggests reading *Hamlet* as a tragedy of hesitation, not only of the vertigo before the fall of which Marcellus speaks and which Horatio fears the young man will take when the Ghost lures him to the watery abyss, but all others as well, especially the biblical fall from grace into crime and desire.[65] This imaginary order of precipitation is not always restituted by translators. It is, however, to this fall that Claudius refers when he tries to pray:

> And what's in prayer but this two fold force,
> To be forstallèd ere we come to *fall*
> Or pardoned being *down*? Then I'll look *up*.
> (III, iii, 48–50, Nemer's emphasis)

Not only François-Victor Hugo but even Bonnefoy, Nemer points out, are inattentive here and the latter displaces the whole of the metaphor in the abstract light of its meditative signification:

> Et la prière, n'est-ce pas la vertu double
> Qui peut nous retenir au bord de la faute
> Ou nous vaut le pardon? Je pourrais relever le front.
> (p.115)

> [And does not prayer have this double virtue
> That can restrain us on the brink of sin
> Or win us pardon? I could raise my head.]

However, Nemer herself conceptualizes space in essentialist terms. She omits to note that for Bonnefoy, the idea of a fall is of something which meets no resistance of any kind (sin?). This can be seen more clearly in Hamlet's desire "To die; to sleep; no more" (III, i, 64–5) where the lure of an unopposed fall is accompanied by the vision of some ill-defined Nirvana: a world all of light and free from space and time – in his own poetry Bonnefoy will come to the awareness (as will Hamlet) that our being exists neither in light nor in darkness alone, but in light and darkness together. Bonnefoy's (and Hamlet's) "readiness" lies in the acceptance of the "ceaseless resurgence of hope based on nothing."[66] Therefore the concept of space is not essential to Bonnefoy's basically global, gnostic outlook on translation.

The 1988 *Hamlet* is more concrete, straightforward, and resourceful in its attempts to put Bonnefoy's translation poetics into practice than the 1962 version. Perhaps a better definition for Bonnefoy's economy of expression than essentialism is that it represents a tendency towards allegorization and spiritualism in the manner of the Imagists, who borrowed minimalist techniques from the haiku. To an extent, Bonnefoy's translation strategy is contradictory and the result of a deconstructionist tendency which at the same time veers toward the spiritual. Because of this, some of the strategies he uses can be interpreted as both clarifying and allegorizing or mysticizing the original. The fact that Bonnefoy's translation poetics produces a text which retains so much of Shakespeare's multireferentiality leaves any theatre director many options with which to work. If it is true that Bonnefoy's translation chooses not to highlight the spatial dimension of *Hamlet*, Patrice Chéreau's 1988 direction of the play in Avignon and later in Nanterre emphasized the space, the height, the depth, darkness and light, which, combined with Bonnefoy's multireferential text, produced a *Hamlet* very close to the original Elizabethan "total theatre" that is supposed to have been performed at the Globe.[67]

Chéreau's *Hamlet* was designed to be a feast for the senses. Bonnefoy's rhythmic text was performed to the accompaniment of the director's quasi-Wagnerian combination of eerie music (used to warn of the arrival of the Ghost, who, in Avignon at least, was mounted on a gray horse with flowing mane and evil demeanor), light, and space. The text was performed uncut and ran for almost five hours, punctuated by the reappearance of the riding Ghost, and the music as a leitmotiv.

Perhaps the most notable aspect of the performance, though, was the staging. The play was given outside, in the courtyard of the Palais des Papes in Avignon, which encircled the playing area much like an Elizabethan "public" theatre would have done (and which recalls Elsinore castle). Like the Elizabethan stage, which was seen from three sides and was raised from 4 to 6 feet to improve the view for the standing spectators and to provide understage space for trapdoors and special effects (of which there were many in this production), Chéreau's stage was a raised (though unroofed) platform with sets of columns on the sides, dividing the stage space vertically (as in the Elizabethan theatre). The compensating feature for there being no "heavens" or apparent (physical) discovery space was the stage's ability to create its own space as and when needed. The columns in fact formed part of a pseudo-constructivist woodwork mechanism which enabled the columns themselves or the front of the stage to rise and fall, thus creating a multilevel playing area which allowed for the exploitation of the spatial metaphors still identifiable in Bonnefoy's translation. The empty space of the stage, its ability to create different playing levels, and the use of columns and a raised stage echoed the dynamics of the Elizabethan public theatres and kept the audience's attention firmly on the play.

Space was created in several ways by Chéreau. The "To be or not to be" soliloquy was performed on a darkened stage with Hamlet entrapped by a circle of light, alone and hesitant before the dark forces of the world which surround him. The dumb show and the "Mousetrap" were both performed in a pit formed by the sunken forestage, and Nemer's imaginary order of precipitation was graphically depicted by Claudius, who actually fell face down on the floor when unable to pray.

Perhaps the most novel feature of Chéreau's interpretation of the spatial imagery, though, was to have Polonius hide below stage in the arras scene (using a concealed trap). Hamlet's dagger struck the old man below ground as he plunged it into the stage, and the body was hoisted upward symbolically onto the stage in the revelation scene. At this point the Ghost also emerged from below, and with the accompanying musical leitmotiv, Chéreau managed to stir his audience.

Chéreau's objective in staging Bonnefoy's *Hamlet* was to entertain his audience for a full five hours with a combination of innovative stage effects, a brilliantly choreographed and extremely physical duel between Hamlet and Laertes, a goodly mix of comedy (Hamlet making Yorick's skull tell jokes, gravediggers with Belgian accents), suspense, and old-fashioned melodrama (the Ghost mounted and appearing to musical accompaniment), all made possible by a French translation which, by its allegorical thrust, empowered the director to actualize the Elizabethan original.

Bonnefoy's essays bring out his conception of *Hamlet* as a play of inherent contradictions: presence and absence, life and death, the tangible and the spiritual, the clear and the obscure. At times Hamlet evokes Bonnefoy's own poetics perfectly as in the second scene of Act II:

> Quel chef-d'oeuvre que l'homme! ... La merveille de l'univers, le parangon de tout ce qui vit! Et pourtant que vaut à mes yeux cette quintessence de poussière?
>
> (p.74)
>
> (What a piece of work is a man ... the beauty of the world, the paragon of animals! And yet to me what is this quintessence of dust?)
>
> (II, ii, 303–8)

One could of course read into this an extended analogy of the human race and all its works, of Bonnefoy and Shakespeare, of their respective *Hamlets*, of wo/man being created, wo/man belonging to Creation and wo/man being creative. Will Bonnefoy's poetry lead him to a work hailed as "la merveille de l'univers" or as "la quintessence de poussière"?

As Richard Stamelman points out, Bonnefoy uses a

> poetics of decentering... to make the omnipresence of alterity visible in his writing and also to avoid the coherence, closure and finality all poetic forms create.... At any moment, the text can unwrite itself, for the most completed, finished work, according to Bonnefoy, is at once a "new text and a new disavowal of the new text."[68]

Here Bonnefoy's allegorical aesthetics of revision reaches its dialectical resolution. It is precisely in the allegory of decay that allegory reveals its own limits, for here "decay is not so much signified, represented allegorically, as itself significant, offered as allegory – the allegory of resurrection."[69] As in Benjamin's theory of allegory, it is not until the last moment that the whole nihilistic technique of destructive contemplation turns in on itself. Allegory is allegorized by reality; the allegorist awakens in God's world, a terrestrial paradise of things and beings.

The fact that Bonnefoy felt the need to work on five separate editions of *Hamlet* at the rate of one per decade (excluding the re-edition of 1959) suggests that as a poet/translator, he is quite simply obsessed with the immense quality of the text. Not only has Bonnefoy produced multiple translations of *Hamlet*, he has also written several articles on the problems of translating Shakespeare from a French perspective. His constant return to the play further implies a continuous interplay between the rewriting of his *Hamlet* translations and his own poetic output. Not only is he glorifying *Hamlet* and working for the continuous canonization of this text for the twentieth century, but in openly writing of his own translation practices as opposed to and in opposition to those of his predecessors, he is seeking to persuade his readers and critics to accept the allegorization of his own translation of *Hamlet*.

Chapter 6

Theatre as translation/Translation as theatre
Shakespeare's Hamlet by the Théâtre du Miroir

Today, at the end of the twentieth century, the playwright whose works are performed most often in French theatres is William Shakespeare. There has, over the course of the last fifty years, been a singular renewal of interest in the work of a man who was born four centuries ago. If one looks at theatre history, it becomes obvious that for a century, at least in Europe, Shakespeare has been a leading *agent provocateur* in many theatrical revolutions: from Copeau to Reinhardt, from Giorgio Strehler to "Avignon," nothing has been done, undone, or redone without him. In the last fifty years Shakespeare has been produced about as often as Molière and more often than Racine on the French stage. In France, Shakespeare productions seem to have been attempted by absolutely everyone, from provincial government-subsidized companies seeking to fill their theatres to the avant-garde. During the 1976–7 theatrical season, for example, there were no fewer than seven separate productions of *Hamlet* in France.

Of all of Shakespeare's plays, *Hamlet* is perhaps the most famous, the most classic of classic plays. *Hamlet* it was that in 1977 seemed to haunt the collective French theatre consciousness. Three separate *Hamlets* were performed in Paris in the month of November alone: two in French (directed by Benno Besson and Daniel Mesguich) and one in Russian (directed by Yuri Lyubimov), each highlighting a different character, a different way of being and of dreaming. Hardly brothers, almost strangers, these three *Hamlets* are linked only by a vague resemblance to each other, as is the case with so many separate translations of the same original. Nevertheless, none of the three directors totally abandoned the original. They all made cuts, but a contemporary audience's attention span was the main reason behind their decision, rather than a desire to "bowdlerize" the text. In all three versions Shakespeare's text remains recognizable, although there are numerous variants.[1] The impression of heterogeneity has been rendered more radically, and one wonders whether or not the play's own remarkable history and reception over the years are not the root cause of this.

Daniel Mesguich, who produced his 1977 *Hamlet* for the Théâtre du Miroir, was asked by a French critic, Gervais Robin, why he felt the need to produce another *Hamlet* or indeed another classic, given the proliferation of such revivals at the time.[2] His reply was that such a question is based on the assumption that to produce yet another *Hamlet* is to reduplicate all previous *Hamlets*, that any "originality" sought by the director, or the translator for that matter, could only be "originality" in the bourgeois sense, that is to say that any new shade of meaning the director (and translator) could possibly impart would have to do with the main character of the play, the storyline, or better still, the theme that is developed throughout. This assumption in turn relies on an instrumentalist notion of writing, where the text is closed with a single meaning, recognized by everyone. Such a question also presupposes that there can only be one definitive translation and/or performance of any text, a neutral, transparent translation and *mise en scène* that faithfully render the canonized "meaning" of a text, a notion which in its turn rests on an instrumentalist conception of translation and theatre as a negation of both translation and performance as signifying practices. If reinterpretation is useless, if *Hamlet* has but one definitive meaning known to all, and if it is only possible for one translation and one production of a text to carry this meaning, then the original question becomes absolutely absurd: one ends up repudiating the notion of a repertory of classics in the theatre altogether.[3]

Therefore the question raised by a seventh production of *Hamlet* within a year should not be "Why put on a production and a translation of *Hamlet* when there have already been six others this year?" but rather "Why bother producing *Hamlet* today at all, when the play has already been performed in the past, when everyone already knows the story because it is a classic?" That is to say, "Why produce and translate a classic, particularly the classic?" Mesguich has addressed himself to these questions in some detail in several interviews.[4] It becomes obvious that *Hamlet* is the archetypal classic text for him, and that this is neither fortuitous, nor accidental, nor contingent, but essential to his decision to produce the play in the first place. According to Mesguich, when staging a classic, particularly *Hamlet*, one stages "the fact that it is a classic" before one even faces the problems of staging the play *Hamlet* proper. Therefore the original question, "Why choose *Hamlet?*" implies the underlying double question: if choosing to stage *Hamlet* is choosing to stage a classic, why stage a classic, and of all the classics available, why stage *Hamlet?*

In order to answer the first of these questions it is necessary to ask a further question: what is a classic? Mesguich's answer to this "classic" question is that the definition of a classic text is that it is not one, but two texts. The first text is the materially visible, readable text, the one signed "Shakespeare" or "Racine," having been edited and re-edited. The second text, which is most often unwritten and sometimes unspoken, consists of the interpretative layers which, over the years, have been and continue to be grafted onto the original text: commentaries, analyses, past productions, and critical receptions, stereotypical images – such as the one French *lycéens* have of Laurence Olivier holding a skull in the palm of his hand, inspired by the cover of the popular Garnier-Flammarion edition of the play. By its very nature the second text remains open-ended. It is the sum of the "classicization" of the first. Hence any production of a classic must stage at one and the same time the play and its accompanying baggage of previous interpretation to the point where there is constant interplay between source text and secondary literature.[5] The staging of a classic play, however, will always omit some part of the original performance which is missing as text. It is one thing to perform a text, but there is no text of a performance, so one can never claim to have given the ultimate interpretation of a classic play. Furthermore, the staging of a classic text asks questions of the text written by the father (that is to say Shakespeare) – so as to determine why it belongs to the modern-day repertory. It analyzes the patrimony left to the contemporary director (the Latin *patrimonium* means "gift of the father") and its ascension to celebrated paternity over other texts – its place in the canon. At the same time, however, the father (the play/Shakespeare) interrogates the son (the director/translator) who is in turn forced to question his own interrogation of the father. Thus, if a director stages a classic, the theatre production is violently questioned and compelled to lower its mask, to unveil what constitutes it. In other words, Mesguich believes that the production of a classic is necessary since it questions both its paternal function (its place in the canon) and that which eternalizes it, thereby forcing the production to stage and question itself.

In a sense, both theatre and translation start with death; of the father, of course, the author. Both theatre and translation are signifying practices which are "titillations" put into play by and drawing upon the absence of the main character, the "other," the author. The author, in this case Shakespeare, has left just enough behind with which to replace him, something to render his absence obsessive. To put into question a classic play's place in the canon, to lay bare the meaning of a text and its accompanying history, to exhaust the interrogation of our memory up to the interrogation of meaning itself – that is Mesguich's project and his reason for choosing to stage a classic text, a project which he considers to be the most urgent political gesture open to a contemporary theatre director.

Mesguich defers talking specifically of *Hamlet* the play, because he considers it to be impossible to talk of this classic text without reifying or substantiating it. In his opinion, contrary to other classic texts, *Hamlet* consumes itself completely in the fact that it is a classic text.[6] There is no difference between the fact that it is a classic, and the text of the play itself. Nevertheless the ultra-famous aspect of the play finally seduced Mesguich to stage the classic of all classic plays, the text of all texts, the Bible of the theatre. Moreover, Mesguich considers *Hamlet* to be a play about theatre. If its main character displays a melancholic nature, this is because he is aware that he is but a character in the play. Beyond this reading, Mesguich professes not to interpret the play.[7] He proclaims that he is against interpretation, at least against the kind of interpretation that reduces a complex play to a single, unified meaning or to an authorial message. Yet both in interviews with Mesguich and in his production of the play, the reader and spectator can easily spot the influence of such French critics as Barthes, Lacan,

Derrida, and Sibony. Moreover, not only is Mesguich directing a French translation of Shakespeare's *Hamlet*, but he also makes it clear that his *Hamlet de Shakespeare* is a translated play. *Le Hamlet de Shakespeare* appears to be a play about theatre as well as a play about translation.

What should a modern French translation of Shakespeare's *Hamlet* strive to be (or not to be)? Most certainly not a translation in modern French dress. What is innovative about Michel Vittoz's translation, according to Mesguich, is that it does not translate the old into the new, but that it takes into account the fact that *Hamlet* is a classic text, and that a classic text consists of two texts.[8]

Vittoz wrote his translation specifically for Mesguich's *mise en scène*. Having worked for several years with the company of the Théâtre du Miroir, he incorporated their theories of theatre into his translation, which also consists of two texts. There is a first translation, a translation of Shakespeare's text in a language that would be contemporary to that of Shakespeare, that is to say a translation of seventeenth-century English into French of the same period. But Vittoz's seventeenth-century French is fictitious (*fictif*), a language of pleasure (*de plaisir*) in which the archaisms need not necessarily be genuine to ring true.[9] The challenge (*la gageure*), according to Mesguich, is to write a pseudo-Elizabethan text, say a play signed "Guillaume Branlelance" of which Shakespeare's text would be only the translation, and strangely enough, the only translation in English. There is a second translation which consists of the first, or the original text, but supplemented by the historical layers that have covered it ever since the fictitious date of its production. This second translation reflects the thoughts of Mallarmé, Joyce, Ernest Jones, Sibony, Freud, and Mao.[10] It also explicitly recognizes that the French language has evolved and that it is still in the process of changing. It "translates" French into French, it translates from François-Victor Hugo, André Gide, and Yves Bonnefoy, thus placing itself within (and against) the French translation tradition of *Hamlet*. Horatio, for instance, being a student, has obviously read the traditional Western canonical works, including *Hamlet*. His line, "That can I. At least the whisper goes so" (I, i, 79–80), is rendered by Vittoz as: "Je le puis, tel est du moins le bruit qui court, là comme Gide l'a traduit" (p.5 ms) [That I can, at least rumor has it so, just like Gide translated it].[11] But his text does not translate: "Des mots, des mots, des mots" (p.31 ms) ("words, words, words" (II, ii, 193)); or: "Fragilité ton nom est femme" (p.10 ms) ("Frailty thy name is woman" (I, i, 146)); or even: "Etre ou ne pas être" (p.39 ms) ("To be or not to be" (III, i, 56)), since it recognizes the fact that these fragments have become established in the French repertory. Hence this second translation seems to have been created by different translators from different times and finds itself in permanent contradiction as it continuously reactivates its heterogeneous material. In short, Vittoz's translation reflects the oscillation between the past and the present of the *mise en scène*. His "Hamlette" (an omelette of *Hamlet* which spreads in all directions, and a pun on Lacan's notion of "homelette") combines seventeenth-century and modern syntax, archaic expressions and modern slang, quotations from Mallarmé, Joyce, Gide, Bonnefoy, and Lacanian word-play. It offers us both an imaginary French version of Shakespearian language and, simultaneously, our own perception of it.

When Mesguich commissioned Vittoz's translation he wanted each word to brim with significance; his purpose was to multiply meaning in order to give the actors the richest possible material with which to perform. In broad terms, the first act is the one which has been worked through most with archaisms. In the second act Vittoz develops another kind of syntax that is basically not archaic though quite complicated when it follows Shakespeare's syntax. It refers to contemporary texts, to a (dis)organization of the phrase which produces a plurality of meaning. The rest of the play is made up of an interweaving of these two kinds of syntax; a strategy that culminates significantly in Claudius' prayer as if the translator were begging the Bard for forgiveness for his blasphemy:

Merci mon cher Seigneur.
    O faute putrescente, ta puanteur atteint le ciel. La plus antique, la première malédiction pèse sur elle. Le meurtre d'un frère, prier? ...
    Je ne puis combien qu'à mon désir ma volonté s'aiguise. Ce m'est grande force au vouloir mais je me sens coupable plus fortement encore et comme l'homme vers deux tâches se déchire, entre l'une ou l'autre j'hésite et toutes deux néglige.

Quoi, maudite main serais-tu tant croutée du sang de mon frère comme à doubler ton volume n'y aurait-il assez de pluie en la clémence des cieux pour te laver et comme neige blanchir? De quoi serait miséricorde faire qu'elle ne se dresse face à l'offense, et quoi se tient en la prière hors cette double force prévenant la chute de qui se tient à son bord dans le temps qu'elle relève qui serait chût. Lors, je porte mon regard vers les cieux. Ma faute est commise, ô dieu, en quelle forme prier qu'aide me puisse venir.

(pp.54–55 ms)

[Thank you, dear Lord.

Oh, putrescent sin, your stench reaches the sky. The first, most ancient curse hangs over it. A brother's murder; pray?...

How I wish my desire would sharpen my will (to do so). I wish I could, with all my strength, but I feel my guilt even more strongly, and like the man who facing two tasks tears himself apart between one and the other, I hesitate and neglect both of them. What, vile hand, are you so encrusted with my brother's blood that you have doubled in size, so that even the clemency of the skies could not provide enough rain to wash you and bleach you white as snow? What is forgiveness to do, if it cannot face up to the offense, and what use is prayer if not to provide a double indemnity against the downfall of whomsoever stands ready to pray while it picks up those who would have fallen. So I look toward the Heavens. My sin is committed, oh Lord, how should I pray so that help may come to me?]

Indeed in the text of *Hamlet* there is a constant overlapping of all the characters: in terms of their situation and diction they all begin to look alike in one way or another. This is the effect of the dream: there is ongoing condensation and displacement. One soon finds out that Hamlet speaks in the voices of Laertes, Polonius, and Fortinbras, that the character Hamlet is all characters, that he is only the name of the play. Hamlet does not exist, but there remains a book, hence Vittoz's published translation is entitled *Hamlet: Le Livre*. As for the allusions in Vittoz's translation: since the Prince of Denmark does not exist, it is normal that he has read both Mallarmé's comments on the play and Gide's translation and that he says so. Both Mesguich and Vittoz speak of a text (translation) as the pre-text of a performance (*spectacle*) and of a performance (*spectacle*) that takes into account several glosses and commentaries of the original text, since one must put everything on stage.¹² The combination of Vittoz's translation and Mesguich's production precludes any linearity of form and attempts to make us read and hear the shifts in meaning.

Moreover, Vittoz's translation plays with and on words. This verbal playfulness seeks less to produce laughter than to cause the signifier to speak in ways familiar to all Lacanians: willful mistranslation and heavily exploited punning (which may or may not take the form of a hoax) are all presented to us as being pregnant with meaning.¹³ There are also times when the production and the translation deliberately take on a false meaning in order to overcome meaning as such, as in the expression "prendre l'air (l''r') ou ne point le prendre" (p.32 ms) which is an approximate quotation from Tän Rilde saying that the word is death without appearing to be so and which the actor impersonating Polonius dutifully explains in a pedagogical way.¹⁴ A similar borrowing, "lisant au livre de lui-même" (p.30 ms) [reading the book of himself], is taken from Mallarmé and is developed from Mesguich's conception of acting.¹⁵ Another example is that of Polonius as an abusive and voyeuristic father, asking the king and queen "puis-je me Père-mettre" (p.30 ms) [allow me] ("O, give me leave" (II, ii, 170)) when he wishes to intercede and question Hamlet. Still another significant pun is "Je ne serai Laertes que pâle fleuret de ton reflet" (p.86 ms) [of your blade, Laertes, I shall be but ghostly glint] ("I'll be your foil, Laertes" (V, ii, 249)). Neither Mesguich nor his players attempt to project themselves or their own problems into the classic text, in line with Barthes' reflections on Racine.¹⁶ Paradoxically it is the classic text which projects itself into all who come in contact with it: the words "To be or not to be" are a part of everyone's subconscious.

Vittoz's translation mirrors Latin constructions, lexical or syntactical archaisms ("oncques" (p.21 ms) [never], "remembrance" (p.20 ms) [memory], "fieffé gredin" (p.21 ms) [arrant knave]), as well as quotations from modern texts. Sometimes it follows an English syntax and exploits interferences from English. In general, it adopts an eminently modern syntactical (dis)organization. Halfway between Ronsard and Mallarmé, Maurice Scève and Lacan, it seems to belong to no particular time period, being no more Shakespearian than modern. It is in permanent contradiction with itself, operating on different registers, ceaselessly underscoring its heterogeneity. It does not seek to pinpoint meaning but to defer it, not to unify the text but to differentiate it. Its difference from other translations is not limited to this double polarity of archaism and modernity. It mixes up registers, linguistic levels, and even languages. A cascade of archaic words sweeps along a torrent of everyday words (Polonius is called a "vieux con" (p.32 ms) [old bastard]), Lacanian word games, untranslated English words (when the Ghost appears), fragments of sentences taken from foreign translations (when Ophelia goes mad she speaks in tongues), and allusions to previous translations, to significant glosses, and to prestigious interpretations of Hamlet's role make the play text ever more striking.

The significant feature of Mesguich's production is the way he exploits Vittoz's translation. The fact that it was created along with the production, and that the whole work was the product of a close collaboration with the director, makes it impossible here to dissociate translation from performance. Mesguich himself points out that the translation is already an initial *mise en scène* and that the act of translation appears as part of the overall spectacle in his production.

Mesguich's whole production is based on an etymological pun between the words *spectre* and *spectacle*. He does not believe for a second that the play revolves around the central character of Prince Hamlet. In fact Mesguich claims to see three Hamlets in *Hamlet*: the book Hamlet reads is *Hamlet* the play, in its entirety, which itself is composed of the father and the son (one could add the Holy Spirit or the *Witz*, Freud's notion of the joke).[17] Instead of seeing the Ghost on the ramparts at the beginning of the production, Mesguich's Hamlet sees *Hamlet* the play (the father). It should be pointed out that instead of the Ghost, selected parts of *Hamlet* the play in its original, "unadulterated" English version, constantly question the action of the version of the son (the director Mesguich), by being acted out in advance of the corresponding scene in French, in a small re-creation of a theatre at the side of the main stage. Mesguich and company begin with the notion of the French word *spectre*, a Ghost of the father in chains and covered by a white sheet, and transform it into *spectacle*. They replay the original *spectacle* of Hamlet as the *spectre* which questions their own *spectacle*. The original generates the French version: what allows *Hamlet* the play to be performed is the play *Hamlet*.

Similarly, whoever wishes to translate *Hamlet* has to become a Hamlet of sorts and tremble with holy terror in front of a text which represents the Ghost of Hamlet's past (and past *Hamlets*). Vittoz has been forced to translate from Elsinore, but he has not been content to add one more stone humbly to the edifice, for the small credit it may earn him in the eyes of others for being faithful to the father. Vittoz is aware of the absence of the father, but what he really wants to do is to expose the father as a cultural object. His translation will not attempt to define Shakespeare's meaning but to multiply it.

Following Mesguich's theoretical approach, the first scene of *Le Hamlet de Shakespeare* functions as a microcosm of the whole play. This scene shows the guards on lookout duty on the ramparts. They see the Ghost of Hamlet's father, also named Hamlet. In Mesguich's production, the Ghost is equated with the play, *Hamlet*. The scenery is set up as follows: a small baroque theatre, in ruins, is situated stage right, complete with a red velvet curtain for the discovery space and adjoining box seats. Apart from this, the stage is bare (albeit surrounded by mirrors on three walls).[18] When Bernardo, Marcellus, and Horatio see the Ghost, the curtain of the small stage opens to reveal the play *Hamlet* in progress. This "play within the play" is several moments in advance of the play being performed on the large stage. The scene Bernardo, Marcellus, and Horatio can see therefore shows the end of the very scene they are now playing themselves, after the Ghost exits. In other words, they are hearing the lines that they themselves will have to deliver in a few seconds. Horatio, looking out over the ramparts of Elsinore in the fog and darkness, can see himself, his double or mirror image. As Judith Gershman recalls, in the production she saw

> Marcellus says: "Brise-toi ma langue, thee off look where, it comes again [sic]." When the Ghost appears, language breaks down, and a ghost text (i.e. Shakespeare's English in fractured fragments) also appears. This is, in part, what Mesguich calls the "Hamlet effect."[19]

Mesguich reacts against the old-world concept of theatre by staging "realist" theatre (in a Brechtian mold?), showing real actors on a real stage, and so on. In this "realistic" theatre actors are allowed to make a mistake, forget their lines (have a *trou de mémoire*), thereby underscoring the greatest difference between film and theatre, also put into play in Mesguich's *Hamlet*. Yet Mesguich also tries to create a *distanciation chaude* (an active alienation or distancing effect) in his theatre: the actors do not merely (coldly) produce linguistic signs. They must play the fiction (of the character) to give themselves the power suddenly to break it: another oscillation, in a way, from past (psychological theatre) to present (non-psychological theatre).

In Lacanian terms, the text is the law, the father. Hence, the Ghost (the past), the representation of Prince Hamlet's father, is the play *Hamlet*. When the Ghost disappears, the curtain of the little stage closes, the father is once again repressed, and the play continues. The first scene sets the parameters of the *mise en scène*: a *mise en abîme*, literally and figuratively, an infinite series of reflections, a play within a play or, pictorially, a mirror image supported by the mirrors on the stage.[20]

Vittoz explains that the "ghost text" brings panic and wild turmoil in its wake. Mesguich adds that whenever the Ghost appears the (French) text blenches, the blood flows out of it, and one is left with its bare bones: the original English text. The Ghost makes its first appearance before the translation has had a chance to get into gear, and therefore it slips, coughing and spluttering. It reveals itself as a translation, it affirms its status. In other words, what Mesguich stages is the draft of a translation, the overall transferral process of material from one natural language to another. This resembles the initial level of adjustment a play must make to become a stage production: the transformation of the written word into the spoken word, of stage directions into movements and visual effects. It mirrors the challenge of turning source text into translation.[21]

By having the actors first play out (English) lines of Shakespeare's text on the small stage and then having them play lines of Vittoz's French text on the large stage, Mesguich underlines the fact that he is staging the process of translation. Translation, like theatre, is seen as a game, to be approached in a playful manner. The game or the challenge of representing a text onstage is made possible by the fact that underlying meaning is revealed through a series of gaps in the text. The challenge for the director/translator is to exploit those gaps or fissures in the text, to uncover the meanings behind them.

Mesguich qualifies *Hamlet* as a haemorrhagic text, i.e. one which exudes meaning.[22] By using snippets of the original English *Hamlet* on the small stage to generate its own translation on the large stage, he forces the confrontation of the two *Hamlets*, which clash due to the chronological discrepancy of events. The English version is necessarily in advance of its French relative. Likewise, the actor has to create a role knowing full well that all his or her lines have already been created in advance of events on the stage. In the theatre there is always this time lag between the written and the spoken word. Mesguich is just forcing the confrontation of the two for the purpose of theatricality and to underline that his is a text-based theatre, and therefore also a text-generated play. Acting, according to Mesguich, is performed and all meaning generated in a space corresponding to something like an air pocket between the written and the spoken elements of a text. If the actors allow the pocket to burst, that is to say if the written and spoken elements of their roles are allowed to come together, they find themselves blocked; there is no more space in which to generate meaning since the pocket has ceased to exist. More commonly it is said that the actor has *un trou de mémoire* (his or her memory fails). Mesguich has his actors stage this predicament.

Translators can face a similar dilemma in trying to find "le mot juste." They too resort to improvisation and rehearsal, a phenomenon Mesguich exposes on the stage. For him theatre comes down to a business of interstices and the knowledge of how to organize them, how to make the *spectacle* gravitate around them: the "chasm" represented by the prompter's box, gaps in the memory, the "black hole" of the house. Similarly the translator faces these textual interstices and in the ongoing process of making the actual translation he or she improves or rehearses solutions. Given an overall plan, a translator tries something, then tries something else, and sees what works best. Sometimes he or she needs to go back and rework certain things from the beginning: sometimes a slight adjustment of a word or a phrase or an emphasis will make everything flow.[23]

An ingenious addition to Mesguich's representation of *Hamlet* is the character of Yorick the jester.[24] He sticks to his clownish role, but he is very much alive. When he speaks, his speech consists of a rumbling noise, pure gibberish. He appears as a babbling clown and is used as a kind of master of ceremonies. His aphasia affords him a critical distance from the play as a cultural object. Whereas he can only produce inaudible squeaks and grunts for most of the play, at the end he finally manages to pronounce the word "tout" which he proceeds to yell out like a small child who has just learned a new word. He finally says "tout bi" (To be?), and then runs off into the wings, leaving just enough time for the audience to understand, during the ensuing burst of laughter, that it is a play on the famous quotation, and that this fool is throwing back to the public the image of its own buried store of quotations. Having become his own gravedigger in the cemetery scene, he presides clownishly over the rite of the unearthing of the skulls, which have been replaced in this production by theatrical costumes.[25] As a character, Yorick demonstrates that the performance does not remain in the imaginary or symbolic order, but steps over into the "real." This a translation can hardly hope to achieve. Because of this dimension of the real and the theatre's capacity to enact its own theatricality, theatre and translation do not overlap. As practical mental endeavors, translation and theatre have a great deal in common. One can think of translations of literary texts – poetry, fiction, plays – not as flawed equivalents in a different language but as productions or performances. One can perceive a translation as a rendition or a "production" of the pre-existing text. One can recognize the kinds of adjustments a text undergoes in translation as well as compare the theatrical touchstones of production, improvisation, and rehearsal. But one cannot imagine translation having access to the real. This also explains that although translation is ephemeral, it usually is not as ephemeral as a theatrical production. Both activities, however, share an element of play.

Because of the double image of the two theatres there are also two Hamlets and two Ophelias. Some of the minor characters have been cut, or their speeches have been given to actors playing other roles. In Part Two of *Le Hamlet de Shakespeare* we find the only scene that has no counterpart in Shakespeare's text. Ophelia speaks a text written by the French author Hélène Cixous, specifically for the production.[26] Mesguich and Vittoz also tried to find a contemporary equivalent of Ophelia's madness. Vittoz chose to construct a text that would replace Shakespeare's rich Elizabethan verse with a collage of phrases in different languages, including English, Swedish, Arabic, slang words, and a prayer recited by a Hebrew.[27] The two Ophelias experience the throes of madness together in a frenzy of languages "That carry but half sense" (IV, v, 7), as a Gentleman says. The Gentleman understands only half of what Ophelia is saying but, as Mesguich wonders, this does not necessarily mean that she is mad. She is, perhaps, speaking another language. She no longer corresponds to the image the Gentleman (the Shakespearian scholar) has of her, therefore he decides that she is mad. The theme of language is carried even further for Ophelia's drowning and death. Ophelia is drowned onstage by the very account of her death which is spoken by her double, who has emerged from the small theatre. It is the story of her own death that she struggles against, trying in vain to swim against the current of this torrent of language, by saying the text backwards.[28]

In representing Ophelia's "madness" as Babel, the confusion of tongues, Mesguich and Vittoz recognize the fact that other translations have been made of this cultural object. Not only do they expose translations beyond their fatherland; they also question the very notion of translation as implying only two languages. Having Ophelia struggle against her death by uttering the text backwards they allude to a different cultural reading and, one could suggest, writing practice. If we had to translate, say a Hebrew or an Arabic text, we would indeed have to proceed in the opposite linear fashion. Furthermore, Ophelia's dying spoken words reflect a narcissistic mirror-writing on her part.

Mesguich's intention is clearly marked from the beginning in his choice of the title. Mesguich calls the play *Le Hamlet de Shakespeare* and not simply *Hamlet*. It is precisely Shakespeare's text, this classic and cultural artifact, that he will stage. For the Théâtre du Miroir, actualization (updating) and historicism are two delusive attitudes. One consists of blocking out the age of the classic text to make it more relevant to a contemporary audience; the other ends up by denying the fact that we live in the modern world and the fact that the idea of the classic is a notion which continues to work on us: one we learn by rote at school, and know without realizing. Both Mesguich and Vittoz, as we have seen, are fond of promoting the possibility of a pluralistic approach, a dynamics of polyphonic voices, substituting a series of multiple visions for a single unified vision of the work. They challenge "interpretation" or one-dimensional readings of the play. However, within the prism of possible readings, this production decides to give pride of place to both a psychoanalytical reading and the Derridean notion of writing. It is structured around a conception of theatre whose key is the metaphor of writing and of the mirror. The materialist wish is to put the self-generation of the text at the centre of their analysis. Both Mesguich and Vittoz regard the text as self-generating, as being at the root of its own origin. The body of the play, the living organism which makes it work is not the character but the written text as a continuum of words, words, words. According to Mesguich a play can be directed if the text is porous enough to allow meaning to seep forth. What defines Mesguich's theatrical practice is precisely the *mise en crise* of classic plays seen in terms of paternal discourse. The classics can be equated with patrimony, the heritage received from a father by a son. If these plays are not performed, if they are not worked upon or rewritten, they will take over and work on us. In certain aspects extremely iconoclastic, totally "unfaithful" to Shakespeare, to tradition, to scrupulous respect for the text, Mesguich's production nevertheless remains even more "faithful" to the ideas of creation and pleasure in the theatre and, we may add, in translation.

Concluding remarks

With Michel Vittoz, Daniel Mesguich, and the Théâtre du Miroir, the point has been reached where the distinction between translation and original is seen to break down. *Hamlet* is no longer presented as a literary work, but as a representation of a multiethnic culture in which national boundaries matter little or not at all. A narrow linguistic model of translation could not hope to describe the effect Vittoz's translation and Mesguich's production had on French theatre.

I have attempted to argue that the only approach to translation equipped to describe successive renditions of a foreign play is the approach outlined in the Introduction, which sees translation in terms of acculturation. Indeed this book as a whole argues not only for the establishment of a cultural model of translation, but for the need to introduce a field of cultural studies to replace altogether the traditional field of the literary study of translation. Linguistic and interpretative literary models are too limited in nature: they cannot open up the necessary number of perspectives to describe translation's effect on the development of literature within a given receiving culture.

With the help of the model sketched in the Introduction, I hope to have thrown some light on the way in which *Hamlet* translations influenced the development of French theatre, as well as the importance of these translations to the personal poetics of some of the translators. This model also makes it possible to trace the development of translational norms in France over the past 200 years. It reveals that for many years French translators did not adhere to the textual, poetic, and theatrical norms operative in the original dramatic text and the source culture in which it was conceived. Ducis and Dumas not only felt obliged to change the verse form, but also felt bound drastically to rework the characterization and the narrative and dramatic structure of the original in their respective *Hamlets*. Neither translator felt able to allow the hero to die, and both used a form of the classical alexandrine throughout, in place of Shakespeare's mixture of verse and prose. Both translations entailed a generic shift: Ducis transformed *Hamlet* into a neo-classical tragedy with overtones of the bourgeois sentimental *drame*, while Dumas presented Shakespeare's original as one of his own romantic dramas, with distinct echoes of melodrama.

Schwob/Morand and Gide chose to adhere to the textual norms of the original, adopting its overall dramatic structure and plot, but rendering Shakespeare's English into French prose. Both versions sought to integrate *Hamlet* into the French *patrimoine*, but in widely divergent ways. Schwob/Morand made use of an antiquated pseudo-seventeenth-century French and French folklore to historicize the play. Gide modernized *Hamlet* in order to make the play relevant to the post-war avant-garde theatre audience.

Bonnefoy fulminates against Gide's audacity in not respecting the philosophical and form-related codes operative in *Hamlet*. In his translation of the play, he seeks to expand French translational norms by positing adherence to the verse form of the original dramatic text as a necessary criterion for the translation of Shakespeare into the receiving culture.

Mesguich, on the other hand, explodes the idea of translational norms. The Vittoz/Mesguich production presents itself as a model of playfulness, suggesting that anything and everything is possible in a theatre which revolves around the notion of translation. Not only does this *Hamlet* stage Vittoz's translation, it also exposes it in a direct comparison with the original dramatic text. The two *Hamlets* (Vittoz's and Shakespeare's) are then joined onstage by a multiplicity of other *Hamlets*: the translation is presented as a collage of previous French versions of the play and various foreign translations of the same text, plus non-Shakespearian material in the form of an insertion specially written by Hélène Cixous.

In Mesguich's *Le Hamlet de Shakespeare* the boundaries separating original and translation are thrown into relief. They resist any attempt on the part of the reader-spectator to make them fit any "transcendent determining instance." The whole notion of translation as "acculturation" is thus laid bare: *Hamlet* is exposed as a cultural object along with our attempts to acculturate the play as an object. Following a strategy of double negation, this translation of a translation is transformed into an original: a play about a play becomes a study in multiethnic reality, an acculturation of an acculturation becomes a representation of culture at large, the world itself, a place of unresolved contradictions that permits the expression of ideas outside the canon of Eurocentric or social logic.

It is fair to say that, without these translations, the history of French theatre would have been very different. Translations of such a seminal nature should therefore be included in any description of the development of a literature.

APPENDIX: TABLE OF SELECTED *HAMLET* PRODUCTIONS

Date	Place	Number of performances in repertory	Translator	Hamlet
September 30, 1769–January 10, 1770	Comédie Française (Rue. des Fossés-Saint-Germain-des-Prés)	12	Ducis	Molé
November 24, 1787–July 4, 1789	Comédie Française (Faubourg Saint Germain)	10	Ducis	La Rive (February 18, 1788) St Fal (July 4, 1789)
April 19, 1803–February 1, 1815	Comédie Française (Rue de Richelieu)	30	Ducis	Talma
October 19, 1815	Opéra	1		(benefit)
October 27, 1815–March 15, 1818	Comédie Française (Rue de Richelieu)	15	Ducis	Talma
August 29, 1818	Opéra	1	Ducis	Talma
September 26, 1818–November 20, 1818	Comédie Française	2	Ducis	Talma
February 20, 1819	Opéra Comique	1	Ducis	Talma
February 23, 1819–May 15, 1823	Comédie Française	18	Ducis	Talma

Date	Venue	Text	Actor(s)	Performances
May 24, 1824–May 23, 1826	Comédie Française	Ducis	Talma	8
December 31, 1826	Comédie Française	Ducis	Victor	1
September 1827	Odéon (Coventry Repertory)	Original text	Kemble	
March 11, 1828–October 12, 1829	Comédie Française	Ducis	Firmin/Geffroy	12
January 18, 1830–June 29, 1851	Comédie Française	Ducis	Messrs Geffroy, Beauvallet, David, Ligier, *et al.*	95
December 1844–January 1845	Salle Ventadour, Paris	Original text	Macready	
December 15, 1847	Théâtre Historique	Dumas–Meurice	Rouvière	
December 1867	Gaîté	Meurice revision	Mme Judith	
(April 28, 1884)	(Admitted to Comédie Française repertory)	(Dumas–Meurice)		
February 27, 1886	Porte St Martin	Cressonois–Samson	Sarah Bernhardt (Ophelia)	
September 28, 1886–May 1, 1890	Comédie Française	Dumas–Meurice	Mounet-Sully	110
1893	On tour London	Dumas–Meurice	Mounet-Sully	
1894	On tour USA	Dumas–Meurice	Mounet-Sully	

Date	Place	Number of performances in repertory	Translator	Hamlet
May 26, 1896–1897	Comédie Française	46	Dumas–Meurice (end includes Fortinbras)	Mounet-Sully
1897–1904	On tour		Dumas–Meurice (end includes Fortinbras)	Mme Dudlay
April 23, 1898	Bouffes du Nord		Dumas–Meurice (end includes Fortinbras)	Mme R. Derigny
May 20, 1899	Théâtre Sarah Bernhardt		Schwob–Morand	Sarah Bernhardt
May 9, 1904	Comédie Française	24	Dumas–Meurice (end includes Fortinbras)	Mounet-Sully
July 20, 1909–April 11, 1911	Comédie Française	21	Dumas–Meurice (11 tableaux, 1/2 hour shorter)	Mounet-Sully
August 8, 1910	Orange, Théâtre Antique	3	Dumas–Meurice (11 tableaux, 1/2 hour shorter)	Comédiens Français
May 18 and 25, 1916	Comédie Française	2	Dumas–Meurice Tableaux 6–9	Lambert

Date	Venue	Adaptation	Director/Lead
December 1920	Geneva	Schwob–Morand	Pitoëff
1924	Comédie Française	Dumas-Meurice	De Max
December 1926	Paris	Schwob–Morand	Pitoëff
November 1927	Théâtre des Mathurins	Schwob–Morand	Pitoëff
(1932)	(Dropped from Comédie Française repertory)	(Dumas-Meurice)	
March 16, 1942	Comédie Française	Guy de Pourtalès	Barrault
September 1942	Théâtre Hébertot	Michel Arnaud	Casadesus
October 17, 1946	Théâtre Marigny	André Gide	Barrault (and dir.)
September 1948	Edinburgh Festival	Gide	Barrault (and dir.)
June 12–20, 1954	Angers, Festival d'Angers	Dumas-Meurice	Dir. Jean Marchat
June 17, 1954	Angers, Festival d'Angers	adaptation Marcel Pagnol	Serge Reggiani (and dir.)
November 1975	Théâtre de la Plaine	adaptation Les Tréteaux du Midi	Dir. Denis Llorca
March 1977	Centre dramatique national, Nice-Côte d'Azur		J.-P. Bisson (and dir.)
March 4, 1977	Maison de la Culture, Grenoble (prod. Centre dramatique national des Alpes)	Michel Vittoz	Garcia-Valdez and Bahon (dir. Mesguich)

Date	Place	Number of performances in repertory	Translator	Hamlet
July 16, 18, 20, 22, 24, 1977	Palais des Papes, Avignon	5	François Bérault	Philippe Avron (dir. Benno Besson)
October 1977	Maison de la Culture, Nanterre		Vittoz	Garcia-Valdez and Bahon (dir. Mesguich)
November 1977	Théâtre des Amandiers, Nanterre (prod. Compagnie du Miroir)		Vittoz	Garcia-Valdez and Bahon (dir. Mesguich)
November 5, 1977–January 14, 1978	Théâtre de l'Est Parisien (TEP) Paris		François Bérault	Avron (dir. Besson)
November 17, 18, 22, 1977	Théâtre National de Chaillot (prod. Moscow Taganka Theatre)	3	in Russian; fragments of Gide translation played to audience over headphones	V. Visotskii (dir. Yuri Lyubimov)
February 1978	Montpellier (prod. TEP)		François Bérault	Avron (dir. Besson)
August 1978	Festival de Saintes, St Etienne			Dir. Daniel Benoin
March 1983	Théâtre de Chaillot, Paris (prod. Yannis Kokkos)		Raymond Lepoûtre	Richard Fontana (dir. A. Vitez)

June 1, 1983	Teatro Garignano, Turin (prod. Comédie de Genève)		dir. Besson
November 24, 1983	Théâtre du Grammont, Montpellier (Théâtre du 80/cie Jacques Weber *et al.*)	Jean-Michel Déprats	François Marthouret (and dir.)
February 1984	Bouffes du Nord, Paris	Déprats	Marthouret (and dir.)
December 26, 1986–January 1987	Théâtre Gérard Philippe, St Denis	Vittoz	Mesguich (and dir.)
April 1987	Nuova Scena, Bologna (prod. Centre dramatique national de St Denis)	Vittoz	Mesguich (and dir.)
July 18, 1988–August 1988	Cour d'honneur du Palais des Papes, Avignon	Yves Bonnefoy	Gérard Désarthe (dir. P. Chéreau)
November 29, 1988–February 11, 1989	Théâtre des Amandiers, Nanterre	Bonnefoy (1988 text)	Jacques Schmidt (dir. Chéreau)
October 1989	Teatro Lirico, Milan (prod. Compagnie de Nanterre-Amandiers)	Bonnefoy	Désarthe (dir. Chéreau)

Notes

INTRODUCTION: A CULTURAL MODEL OF TRANSLATION

1 Raymond van den Broeck, "Vertaalkunst, vertaalkunde, vertaalwetenschap: *After Babel* maakt de verwarring niet ongedaan," *Spectator,* 7 (1977–8): 154.
2 André Lefevere is one of the theorists who has tried to situate translation studies within the general field of literary studies, as well as within comparative literature.
3 André Lefevere, "Translation Studies: The Goal of the Discipline," *Literature and Translation: New Perspectives in Literary Studies*, eds James S Holmes, José Lambert, and Raymond van den Broeck (Leuven, Belgium: ACCO, 1978), 234–5.
4 Hilaire Belloc already talked about translation in these terms in his Taylorian Lecture *On Translation* (Oxford: Clarendon Press, 1931). Lawrence Venuti's essay "The Translator's Invisibility," *Criticism* (Spring 1986), 179–211 which I shall briefly discuss, underlines the low status of the translator in a socio-economic and ideological context.
5 Alexander Fraser Tytler, *Essay on the Principles of Translation*, 1813, intro. Jeffrey F. Huntsman (Amsterdam: John Benjamins, 1978).
6 ibid., 13.
7 ibid., 16.
8 Eugene A. Nida and Charles R. Taber, *The Theory and Practice of Translation* (Leiden: E. J. Brill, 1974).
9 ibid., 14.
10 For further information on the specific problems involved in reviewing a translation, see Felix J. Douma's article "On Reviewing a Translation: A Practical Problem in Literary Criticism," *Meta,* 17.2 (1972): 87–101.
11 Jean-François Ducis, *Oeuvres*, 4 vols (Paris: 1826), vol. 1, *Hamlet.*
12 Marcel Schwob and Eugène Morand, "La Tragique Histoire d'Hamlet," *Oeuvres complètes* VII–VIII (Geneva: Slatkine Reprints, 1985), 1–187.

13 Itamar Even-Zohar, *Papers in Historical Poetics* (Tel Aviv: The Porter Institute for Poetics and Semiotics, 1978). André Lefevere discusses the contribution of the "Tel Aviv/Low Countries School" to translation theory in his article "Poetics (Today) and Translation (Studies)," *Modern Poetry in Translation: 1983*, ed. Daniel Weissbort, introd. Ted Hughes (New York: MPT/Persea, 1983), 190–5. This group of theorists at the Porter Institute for Poetics and Semiotics of the University of Tel Aviv and at the Universities of Antwerp, Amsterdam, and Leuven proposes a functionalist approach to translated literature. In *Papers in Historical Poetics* Even-Zohar, one of the group's chief theoreticians, introduce the concept of literature as a (poly)system which helps to establish a new paradigm for the study of literary translation.
14 Itamar Even-Zohar, *Papers in Historical Poetics*, 45–53.
15 Even-Zohar conceives of culture's main work, in Yuri Lotman's terms, as the structural organization of the surrounding world and sees universals as historical generalizations rather than ahistorical truths (ibid., 40–1). See Yuri Lotman *et al.*, *Theses on the Semiotic Study of Culture* (Lisse, The Netherlands: The Peter de Ridder Press, 1975).
16 Itamar Even-Zohar, *Papers in Historical Poetics*, 26.
17 ibid., 27.
18 ibid., 27.
19 Lefevere criticizes Even-Zohar's introduction of the primary versus secondary opposition as being too much a part of Systems Thinking, and also states that Even-Zohar is being unnecessarily vague by not picking up on the notions of stabilization, polarity, and periodicity contained in Systems Thinking ("Poetics (Today) and Translation (Studies)," 194).
20 Gideon Toury, *In Search of a Theory of Translation* (Tel Aviv: The Porter Institute for Poetics and Semiotics, 1980).
21 ibid., 51.
22 The notion "horizon of expectation," borrowed from Hans-Robert Jauss, can be explained as the frame of reference within which our understanding of a work occurs – it is also the means by which that comprehension is subsumed into a literary and sociological tradition. Robert C. Holub defines this notion as "an intersubjective system or structure of expectations," a "system of references," or "a mind-set that a hypothetical individual might bring to any text" in his book on *Reception Theory: A Critical Introduction* (London: Methuen, 1984), 59. For a critique of Jauss' notion of "horizon of expectations" see Patrice Pavis, *Languages of the Stage* (New York: Performing Arts Journal Publications, 1982), 73–7.
23 Gideon Toury, *In Search of a Theory of Translation*, 57.
24 ibid., 58.
25 Both André Lefevere and Ria Vanderauwera have criticized Toury's "adequate translation" as an "intermediating construct" or model for the comparison of a literary source text and its translation. In his review of the polysystem theory, Lefevere notices "a kind of

creeping essentialism ... in the work of some of its supporters, most dramatically evidenced in the appearance of a 'tertium comparationis' hovering somewhere ... between original and translation" ("Poetics (Today) and Translation (Studies)," 193). Similarly, in her review of Toury's book, Vanderauwera underlines that Toury "unnecessarily complicates his method of analysis by introducing a 'tertium comparationis'" (p.178). She further points out that Toury drops this notion of an "adequate invariant" in the two case studies that conclude his book (p.179). See Ria Vanderauwera, "Review: Gideon Toury in Search of a Theory of Translation," *Dispositio*, 7.19–21 (1982): 177–9.

26 Toury further introduces a descriptive and functional notion of equivalence. Optimal and normative definitions of equivalence cannot serve as a premise for the study of existing translations and translation practices. According to Toury, the notion of equivalence must undergo an essential change: it cannot be a "material" concept any longer; it must become a "functional" concept instead. This functional approach allows Toury to claim that it is not the analyst's task to determine whether an equivalence exists between translation and original, but rather what *type* and *degree* of equivalence there is between them. In other words the analyst presupposes the existence of equivalence in the comparative study of target text and source text, accepts it as a postulate, and then asks "not *whether* the two texts are equivalent (from a certain aspect), but *what* type and degree of translation equivalence they reveal" (*In Search of a Theory of Translation*, 47). Not only is Toury's approach functional-relational, but the traditional notion of equivalence is changed from an ahistorical, largely normative concept to an historical notion intended as an analytical device.

27 James S Holmes, "Describing Literary Translations: Models and Methods," *Literature and Translation: New Perspectives in Literary Studies*, eds James S Holmes, José Lambert, and Raymond van den Broeck, 69–82.

28 In his essay "Describing Literary Translations: Models and Methods," in ibid., 69–82, James S Holmes urges theorists to develop a satisfactory model of the translation process in order to develop methods for the description of existing translations (p.70). He surveys existing models of the translation process and introduces his own "two-map two-plane text-rank translation model." According to Holmes, the translation of texts takes place on two planes: "a serial plane, where one translates sentence by sentence, and a structural plane, on which one abstracts a 'mental conception' of the original text" (p.72). This "mental conception" or "map" is used as a criterion against which each sentence is tested during the formulation of the translation. Holmes' introduction of an abstract text-rank "map" in his two-plane text-rank translation model supersedes the earlier, unsophisticated lexical or sentence-rank serial models. But one "map" does not seem sufficient to model the actual translation process. Holmes therefore proposes a

second map which guides the translator in making decisions on the serial plane. He thus arrives at a two-plane, two-map model (p.73). Within this model he introduces three sets of rules which relate to specific phases of the translation process. These three-rule sets comprise: derivation rules, projection rules, and correspondence rules.

Holmes notes that in actual practice the different phases (as represented by the three sets of rules) are not always separated from each other in time, but there is a great deal of feedback within the translation process. More important, however, is that Holmes does not regard the map of the source text simply as a map of a linguistic artifact. On the contrary, as a map of a linguistic artifact it will include contextual information; as a map of a literary artifact it will contain intertextual information and, as a map of a socio-cultural artifact it will subsume situational information (pp.74–5).

29 James S. Holmes, "Describing Literary Translations: Models and Methods," ibid., 80.
30 Robert de Beaugrande, *Factors in a Theory of Poetic Translating* (Assen, The Netherlands: Van Gorcum, 1978), 13.
31 Jiří Levý, "Translation as a Decision Process," *To Honor Roman Jakobson III* (The Hague: Mouton, 1967), 1171–82.
32 ibid., 1171.
33 ibid., 1172.
34 ibid., 1172.
35 ibid.
36 ibid., 1179. Because of his pragmatic orientation, Levý accounts for the reader's interpretation (actualization or concretization). This concern can be traced back to a previous article of his (written in 1963 but not published in English until 1976), "The Translation of Verbal Art," *Semiotics of Art*, eds Ladislav Matejka and Irwin R. Titunik (Cambridge, MA: MIT Press, 1976), 218–64. Here he primarily emphasizes that "the translator's point of departure should not be the text of the original but rather the ideational and aesthetic values contained therein" (p.225). This implies that translators of literary texts not only construe a "map" or "mental conception" based on the original, but that they also have to take into consideration the reader for whom they are translating. Here again Levý makes it clear to what extent translation is a practice-, goal-, and reader-oriented activity.
37 Holmes acknowledges that he bases this distinction on Lefevere's categories of textuality, intertextuality, and contextuality explained in "The Translation of Literature: An Approach," *Babel*, 16.2 (1970): 75–80.
38 James S Holmes, "Rebuilding the Bridge at Bommel: Notes on the Limits of Translatability," *Dutch Quarterly Review of Anglo-American Letters*, 2 (1972): 65–72.
39 ibid., 68.
40 ibid., 68.

41 ibid.
42 Lawrence Venuti, "The Translator's Invisibility," 179–212.
43 ibid., 188.
44 Barbara Harlow, "From Deconstruction to Decolonization: The Political Agenda of Translation," unpublished paper, Special Session on "Theoretical Perspectives on Translation," MLA Convention, Chicago, December 29, 1985, 1.
45 ibid., 4.
46 Fredric Jameson, *The Political Unconscious* (London: Methuen, 1981), 58.
47 André Lefevere, "Translation Studies and/in Comparative Literature: A Modest Proposal for Joining the Mainstream, at Last," paper, Midwest MLA Meeting, St Louis, November 7–9, 1985, 58.
48 Fredric Jameson, *The Political Unconscious*, 58.
49 André Lefevere, "Translation Studies and/in Comparative Literature," 13.
50 ibid., 14.
51 See Note 22.
52 This model would take issue with Goethe's three linear, chronological stages or epochs of translation as outlined in his *West-Östlicher Divan* (1819), inasmuch as he states that every foreign original must pass through all three stages to become a "Germanized foreigner." The model proposed here does not present its three kinds of translation in any order of importance, chronological or otherwise. Nor do all three methods have to be present in a receiving literature as actualized translations of a source text; inversely, all three can be present at once. For selected extracts from Goethe's writing on translation, see André Lefevere, *Translating Literature: The German Tradition* (Assen/Amsterdam: Van Gorcum, 1977), 35–9.

1 JEAN-FRANÇOIS DUCIS' *HAMLET, TRAGÉDIE IMITÉE DE L'ANGLOIS*: A NEOCLASSICAL TRAGEDY?

1 Pierre Antoine de La Place, *Le Théâtre anglois*, 4 vols, (London: 1745–6).
2 These lines are quoted in Robert Davril's article, "Shakespeare in French Garb," *Shakespeare Jahrbuch*, 92 (1956): 197. Throughout the chapter, translations in square brackets are my own.
3 This is a letter dating from July 1776, to the Comte d'Argental translated and quoted in *Yale French Studies*, 33 (1964), 10 (Voltaire, "A Shakespeare Journal").
4 Mary B. Vanderhoof (ed.) "*Hamlet*: A Tragedy Adapted from Shakespeare (1770) by Jean-François Ducis," critical edn, *Proceedings of the American Philosophical Society*, 97.1 (1953): 88–142.
5 See Paul van Tieghem, *Le Préromantisme* (Paris: Sfelt, 1947), 246–7.
6 Je conçois, Monsieur, que vous avez dû me trouver bien téméraire de mettre sur le théâtre français une pièce telle qu'*Hamlet*. Sans parler des irrégularités sauvages dont elle

abonde, le spectre tout avoué qui parle longtemps, les comédiens de campagne et le combat au fleuret, m'ont paru des ressorts absolument inadmissibles sur notre scène. J'ai bien regretté cependant de ne pouvoir y transporter l'ombre terrible qui expose le crime et demande vengeance. J'ai donc été obligé en quelque façon de créer une pièce nouvelle. J'ai tâché seulement de faire un rôle intéressant d'une reine parricide, et de peindre surtout dans l'âme pure et mélancolique d'Hamlet un modèle de tendresse filiale.

(Quoted in Mary B. Vanderhoof, "*Hamlet*: A Tragedy Adapted from Shakespeare (1770) by Jean-François Ducis," 89)

7 Peter V. Conroy, Jr, "A French Classical Translation of Shakespeare: Ducis' *Hamlet*," *Comparative Literature Studies*, 18 (1981): 8.
8 See ibid. for a detailed discussion of the neoclassical aspects of Ducis' play.
9 All subsequent quotations from Ducis' play will be taken from Mary B. Vanderhoof's critical edition unless otherwise stated. Throughout this book I shall be referring to the New Penguin Shakespeare edition of *Hamlet*, ed. T. J. B. Spencer, introd. Anne Barton (London: Penguin Books, 1980).
10 The background to Le Tourneur's *Hamlet* and the scandal it provoked in literary circles is outlined in Jacques Gury's critical edition of the former's preface to his Shakespeare translations: *P. Le Tourneur: Préface du Shakespeare traduit de l'anglois* (Geneva: Droz, 1990).
11 For a more detailed account of the critical reception of Ducis' *Hamlet*, see Helen Phelps Bailey's book *Hamlet in France: From Voltaire to Laforgue* (Geneva: Droz, 1964).
12 I am indebted to Jürgen von Stackelberg's article "*Hamlet* als bürgerliches Trauerspiel: Ideologiekritische Anmerkungen zur ersten französischen Shakespeare-Bearbeitung von Jean-François Ducis," *Romanistische Zeitschrift für Literaturgeschichte*, 3.1–2 (1979): 122–35, for his observations regarding the bourgeois nature of the play.
13 E. Preston Dargan, "Shakespeare and Ducis," *Modern Philology*, 10.2 (1912), 137–77.
14 ibid., 140.
15 Helen Phelps Bailey, *Hamlet in France: From Voltaire to Laforgue*, 15.
16 Note the use of bourgeois mercantile vocabulary.
17 Jürgen von Stackelberg, "*Hamlet* als bürgerliches Trauerspiel," 131–2.
18 J'ai, dans le cinquième acte, laissé aller mon coeur et mon imagination. Je voudrais qu'il pût paraître beau et qu'il produisit un effet terrible et digne de la tragique [sic]. ... Vite, vite, fixons le manuscrit et puis donnez mon Hamlet. Vous m'enverrez vos réflexions sur le champ.

(Quoted in Sylvie Chevalley, "Ducis, Shakespeare et les Comédiens Français," *Revue d'Histoire du Théâtre*, 16.4 (1964): 327–50; 334)

19 "Il faut que le morceau de fureur soit irréprochable par le style et qu'il soit dans la manière du Dante pour les images et la couleur" (quoted in ibid., 334).

20 Je sais que vous êtes disposés à remettre ma tragédie d'*Hamlet* avec les changements et le nouveau cinquième acte que j'y ai faits avant la fièvre qui me ronge depuis trois mois.... Depuis dix-huit mois j'espérais que le travail que j'ai fait à mon ouvrage pourrait vous devenir utile dans le cours de votre répertoire. Ma maladie m'empêche d'aller vous exprimer mon désir de voir ma tragédie dans son nouvel éclat.
(Quoted in ibid., 335)

21 J'ai relu ce matin mon nouvel acte d'*Hamlet* mis au net hier. Il me semble qu'il est de la même pâte que la petite galette que vous avez fait avaler au public. Je l'ai assaisonné autant que je l'ai pu, de grâce, de pitié, et surtout de terreur.
(Quoted in ibid., 335)

22 For more information on Talma and his preparations for the role, see also Noëlle Guibert, "Talma et la création dramatique," *Dramaturgies: Langages dramatiques* (*Mélanges pour Jacques Schérer*) (Paris: Nizet, 1986): 441–50.

2 ALEXANDRE DUMAS AND PAUL MEURICE'S *HAMLET, PRINCE DE DANEMARK*: TRANSLATION AS AN EXERCISE IN POWER

1 See Lady Juliet Pollock, "The 'Hamlet' of the Seine," *Nineteenth Century*, 20 (1886): 805–14; 807; Fernande Bassan, "L'*Hamlet* d'Alexandre Dumas père et Paul Meurice: Evolution d'une adaptation de 1846 à 1896," *Australian Journal of French Studies*, 19 (1982): 11–31; and Jean Jacquot, "Mourir! Dormir ... Rêver peut-être? *Hamlet* de Dumas-Meurice, de Rouvière à Mounet-Sully," *Revue d'Histoire du Théâtre*, 16 (1964): 407–45; 408.

2 See Fernande Bassan, "L'*Hamlet* d'Alexandre Dumas père et Paul Meurice," 12, and Jean Jacquot, "Mourir! Dormir ... Rêver peut-être?", 407.

3 Jean Jacquot, "Mourir! Dormir ... Rêver peut-être?", 407–8.

4 Fernande Bassan, "L'*Hamlet* d'Alexandre Dumas père et Paul Meurice," 14.

5 ibid., 15.

6 Alexandre Dumas, "Hamlet, Prince de Danemark," *Théâtre complet d'Alexandre Dumas*, vol. XI (Paris: Michel Lévy Frères, 1874). This is the new edition of Dumas' 1847 translation, *Hamlet, Prince de Danemark*, "drame en cinq actes (huit parties), en vers, en société avec M. Paul Meurice," which was produced at the Théâtre Historique, December 15, 1847.

7 See Lady Juliet Pollock, "The 'Hamlet' of the Seine," 811–12.

8 Fernande Bassan, "L'*Hamlet* d'Alexandre Dumas père et Paul Meurice," 17.

9 ibid., 16–17. Lee Johnson's article, "Delacroix, Dumas and *Hamlet*," *The Burlington Magazine*, 123.945 (1981): 717–21, is a most interesting account of Delacroix's paintings of Hamlet and the series of lithographs depicting the play he published in 1843. In Johnson's opinion it was no doubt at the suggestion of Dumas that Rouvière imitated Delacroix's conception of Hamlet (p.718).
10 The editions referred to here are the Penguin edition of *Hamlet* (London: Penguin Books, 1980) and the Michel Lévy edition of the 1847 Dumas translation of *Hamlet* published in 1874 (See Note 6). Since the Dumas version does not provide line numbers, I am referring to the page number. Translations in square brackets are my own.
11 Jean Jacquot, "Mourir! Dormir ... Rêver peut-être?", 414.
12 Lady Juliet Pollock, "The 'Hamlet' of the Seine," 811.
13 Jean Jacquot, "Mourir! Dormir ... Rêver peut-être?", 417.
14 ibid., 417–18.
15 Lady Juliet Pollock, "The 'Hamlet' of the Seine," 807.
16 Fernande Bassan, "L'*Hamlet* d'Alexandre Dumas père et Paul Meurice," 20.
17 Jean Jacquot, "Mourir! Dormir ... Rêver peut-être?", 419.
18 Fernande Bassan, "L'*Hamlet* d'Alexandre Dumas père et Paul Meurice," 20.
19 ibid., 21.
20 Alexandre Dumas and Paul Meurice, *Hamlet, Prince de Danemark* (Paris: Calmann-Lévy, 1886).
21 Jean Jacquot, "Mourir! Dormir ... Rêver peut-être?", 419.
22 Fernande Bassan, "L'*Hamlet* d'Alexandre Dumas père et Paul Meurice," 23; and Jean Jacquot, "Mourir! Dormir ... Rêver peut être?", 421.
23 Jean Jacquot, "Mourir! Dormir ... Rêver peut-être?", 425.
24 ibid., 427–8.
25 ibid., 432.
26 Jean Jacquot's remarkable study (ibid.) contains an exhaustive account of Mounet-Sully's preparation for the role of Hamlet and his subsequent interpretation of the prince on the Parisian stage.
27 Fernande Bassan, "L'*Hamlet* d'Alexandre Dumas père et Paul Meurice," 26.

3 MARCEL SCHWOB AND EUGÈNE MORAND'S *LA TRAGIQUE HISTOIRE D'HAMLET*: A FOLKLORIC PROSE TRANSLATION

1 Alexandre Dumas, *Etude sur "Hamlet" et William Shakespeare* (Paris: M. Lévy, 1867), 16. The original French is as follows: "La pièce ... a obtenu un immense succès. Mme Judith a été rappelée trois fois."
2 Christopher Smith, "Shakespeare on French Stages in the Nineteenth Century," in R. Foulkes (ed.) *Shakespeare and the Victorian*

Age (Cambridge: Cambridge University Press, 1986), 223–39; 224. This article pays particular attention to Sarah Bernhardt's preparation for the role of Hamlet.

3 Throughout this chapter I will be referring to the Slatkine reprint of the 1927–9 Paris edition of Schwob's *Oeuvres complètes* (Marcel Schwob and Eugène Morand, *La Tragique Histoire d'Hamlet, Oeuvres complètes*, VII–VIII (Geneva: Slatkine Reprints, 1985), 1–187) and page reference to this edition. Critics have generally concentrated on Schwob's efforts rather than those of Morand, and I apologize in advance if I should fall into the same practice, it having been difficult to establish Morand's precise part in this translation.

4 Christopher Smith, "Shakespeare on French Stages in the Nineteenth Century," 227.

5 Philippe van Tieghem, "Shakespeare au temps du romantisme," *Les Influences étrangères sur la littérature française* (Paris: Presses Universitaires de France, 1961), 194–8.

6 Marcel Schwob and Eugène Morand, *La Tragique Histoire d'Hamlet*. The introductory pages are indicated by Roman numerals in the text.

7 Schwob notes that Dowden, in the version of *Hamlet* the former is using for his translation, exposed the numerous contradictions which the action of *Hamlet* presents from the point of view of time. He discusses Hamlet's age at some length and concludes that he must be a young man, 20 to 25 years old. Hamlet's *taedium vitae* is a moral vice of youth. He further discusses the famous line where the queen refers to Hamlet as fat and lethargic: "He's fat and scant of breath" (V, ii, 281). Schwob decides, in agreement with others, that one should either read "faint" or "hot" for Hamlet's condition, and prefers the latter solution. The queen observes during the duel what the king had foreseen (IV, vii, 156, in Shakespeare): Hamlet will be hot and thirsty. Schwob then acquaints his readers with the idea that Burbage incarnated a less than athletic Hamlet to explain in part the confusion caused by the line (pp.xviii–xix).

8 "On ne saurait croire combien les expressions et les tournures ont d'analogie dans deux langues arrivées au même degré de formation," "Avant-propos à une traduction de Catulle en vers marotiques," quoted in Jean-Claude Noël, "L'art de traduction chez Schwob et chez Gide," *Revue de l'Université d'Ottawa*, 39.2 (1969): 173–211; 174.

9 This idea of periods to be established in the evolution of languages and of correspondences between them probably came to Schwob in the wake of discussions he had with his uncle, Léon Cahun. See Pierre Champion, *Marcel Schwob et son temps* (Paris: Grasset, 1927), 20–1, and Jean-Claude Noël, "L'art de traduction chez Schwob et chez Gide," 174.

10 Il m'a semblé qu'à l'époque de Catulle, la langue latine était formée au même degré à peu près que, chez nous, la langue

française sous Henri IV ... Du reste, cette analogie, dans ce cas, est fort explicable; au XVIe siècle, comme sous César, la langue de la littérature grecque a fait invasion: on retrouve du grec dans les mots et les idées. C'est ce qui fait qu'à mon avis, Catulle n'est traduisible qu'en vieux français"
(quoted in Jean-Claude Noël, "L'art de traduction chez Schwob et chez Gide", 174)

11 "Les traductions en vers ont mauvaise réputation: ou bien elles conservent la forme et altèrent le sens; ou bien elles conservent le sens et envoient au diable la forme. Les deux méthodes sont également défectueuses" (ibid.).
12 ibid., 178–9.
13 It has been my own personal experience when conversing with native French speakers in southwestern Louisiana that this is indeed the case. The "standard" French spoken in this part of the world today has elements of both sixteenth- and seventeenth century usage in addition to various characteristics common to dialects of northwestern France.
14 Jean-Claude Noël, "L'art de traduction chez Schwob et chez Gide," 179.
15 ibid., 179–80.
16 ibid., 192.
17 ibid., 193.
18 ibid., 194.
19 ibid., 194–5.
20 ibid., 185.

4 THE BLANK VERSE SHALL HALT FOR'T: ANDRÉ GIDE'S *LA TRAGÉDIE D'HAMLET*

1 André Gide (trans.) *Hamlet*, by William Shakespeare, ed. Jacques Schiffrin (Boston: Beacon Press, 1964), 5. Translations in square brackets are my own.
2 André Gide, *Correspondance*, vol. II (Paris: Gallimard, 1968), 260.
3 Jacques Cotnam, "André Gide et le cosmopolitisme littéraire," *Revue d'Histoire Littéraire de France*, 70.2 (1970): 267–285; 268.
4 ibid., 273.
5 ibid., 277.
6 ibid., 278.
7 ibid., 271.
8 Gide argued long and hard against those who trumpeted the merits of French literature while ignoring that of the rest of Europe:

"J'attends toujours je ne sais quoi d'inconnu, nouvelles formes d'art et nouvelles pensées et quand elles devraient venir de la planète Mars, nul Lemaître ne me persuadera qu'elles doivent m'être nuisibles ou me demeurer inconnues,"
(*Prétextes* (Paris: Mercure de France, 1963), 60–1)

[I'm still expecting all kinds of unknown quantities: new forms of art and thought, and even if they come from Mars no Lemaître is going to persuade me that I should hate them or remain ignorant of them.]

9 Helen Watson-Williams, "The 'Hamlet' of André Gide," *Essays in French Literature*, 10 (1973): 40–63; 43.

10 Lorsque nous sommes trop usés à force de rechercher le rare, Shakespeare est notre grand secours pour nous replacer dans la vie, pour nous raviver le coeur et nous faire revoir l'humain ... Shakespeare, à notre époque, passe par une phase d'actualité. Il est en correspondence avec nous. Shakespeare a vécu en effet au milieu des meurtres, des révolutions et des catastrophes, comme nous ... entre l'âge de la Foi perdue et celui d'une Foi pas encore retrouvée. Pendant une maladie du Doute, comme nous.

(*Nouvelles Réflexions sur le théâtre* (Paris: Flammarion, 1959), 54)

11 "Ce ton de vérité, de réalisme, de la poésie shakespearienne" (Comments made to *Combat*, quoted in Jean Jacquot, "Vers un théâtre du peuple," *Etudes Anglaises*, 13.2 (1960): 216–47; 221).

12 "Peut-être bientôt mon esprit retrouvera-t-il quelque vigueur pour des projets plus personnels" (André Gide, letter to Roger Martin du Gard, *Correspondance* II, 248).

13 André Gide, *Journal 1939–1949* (Paris: Bibliothèque de la Pléiade, 1954), 130, entry for September 1, 1942.

14 Trouver la solution à ce problème de mécanique, réparer l'appareil, ajuster la balance, c'est régler les comptes, c'est nettoyer l'homme de ses passions, c'est redonner la santé, c'est venir au secours de la vie qui en sera plus forte: c'est rendre la justice, la Vraie. C'est la véritable mission de l'auteur, c'est fondamentalement la fonction sociale du théâtre.

(*A propos de Shakespeare et du théâtre* (Paris: La Parade, 1949), 23)

15 Justin O'Brien, Introduction in André Gide, *Hamlet*, 3.
16 André Gide, "Lettre-Préface," *Hamlet*, 5–6.
17 ibid., 6–7.
18 All page references to Gide's text refer to the edition of *Hamlet* cited in Note 1.
19 Jean-Claude Noël, "L'art de traduction chez Schwob et chez Gide," *Revue de l'Université d'Ottowa*, 39.2 (1969): 173–211; 181–3.
20 The differences between Gide's approach in producing a so-called clear, playable text, and that of Schwob become clearer if one compares the "To be or not to be" monologue, as Noël (ibid., 187–92) does in his close reading of Gide and Schwob. He notes that Gide uses several inversions, changing the nature and function of the words as well as the mode of the verbs. Gide's translation even changes the nature of the assertions: coordinate clauses become subordinate, which has far-reaching consequences in that coordination suggests a democratic world order, with all social classes on the same level through its use of juxtaposition, whereas subordination infers a more classical, hierarchical world view, by means of hypostasis.

21 ibid., 181.
22 Sometimes Gide tries to convey a quasi-Shakespearian tone when he invests his words with a double meaning. For example, when Hamlet replies to Polonius' request: "Then I will come to my mother by and by. [*Aside*] They fool me to the top of my bent. [*Aloud*] I will come by and by" (III, ii, 390–2), Gide uses a pun on *incontinent* meaning both "forthwith" and "débauché":

> Eh bien! Je vais me rendre incontinent près de ma mère. [*A part*] Tous bêtifient à mon gré, de leur mieux. [*A voix haute*] Je viens incontinent.
>
> (p.161)

[All right! I shall go forthwith to my mother/I'm going to be disrespectful to my mother. [*Aside*] In my opinion they do their best to talk twaddle. [*Aloud*] I'm coming forthwith (understood: disrespectfully).]
23 Justin O'Brien, Introduction, in André Gide, *Hamlet*, 6.
24 Jean-Claude Noël, "L'art de traduction chez Schwob et chez Gide," 201–4.
25 Of course the third mouse in this tale is the one who does not stir in scene i, namely the Ghost (I, i, 10).
26 Ever since the Romantic period there has been a conflict of opinion in France between those who espouse "literary" (faithful) translations of Shakespeare and those who champion "playable," although somewhat "bowdlerized," texts. A lively controversy raged in *Le Monde* in 1955 (August 18 and 28; September 6, 22, and 24, 1955), clearly illustrating the conflict between "literary" translators and translators for the "stage." Yves Florenne, representing the latter group and advertising the Club Français du Livre's new Shakespeare collection, had attacked "university" translators in the following terms: "La meilleure manière de l'assassiner (Shakespeare) étant encore la littéralité, à quoi s'efforcent labourieusement des anglicistes consciencieux" [The best way to ruin Shakespeare is to emphasize literality, something the conscientious anglicists work hard to do]. A Professor Loiseau, of the University of Bordeaux, took up the gauntlet and tried to demonstrate that the "tentative de l'équivalence poétique et dramatique" [movement towards poetic and dramatic equivalence] on the part of some modern translators deserved in no way to be called translation but must be relegated to the category of adaptation. (Quoted in Robert Davril, "Shakespeare in French Garb," *Shakespeare Jahrbuch*, 92 (1956): 197–206; 205–6).
27 Nancy Lee Cairns, "*Hamlet*, Gide and Barrault," in William G. Holzberger and Peter B. Waldeck (eds) *Perspectives on Hamlet*, (Cranbury, NJ: Associated U Presses, 1975), 207–46; 240.
28 ibid., 240.
29 ibid.
30 Une tragédie ne se termine qu'avec *la solution complète, générale, totale* du conflit humain exposé, et non simplement avec la mort

de son héros. Une pièce est une pièce et non pas seulement un rôle; une tragédie ne se termine que grâce au justicier et non pas seulement grâce à la victime.

(Quoted in Jean-Louis Barrault, *Nouvelles Réflexions sur le théâtre*, 96)

5 YVES BONNEFOY'S *LA TRAGÉDIE D'HAMLET*: AN ALLEGORICAL TRANSLATION

1 Unless otherwise indicated all references will be to Bonnefoy's 1988 edition of *La Tragédie d'Hamlet* (Paris: Mercure de France, 1988). The numbers cited will be the page number, not the line number. Translations in square brackets are my own.
2 Bonnefoy published the following *Hamlet* translations: Club Français du Livre (1957), re-edited in 1959, Mercure de France (1962), Gallimard (1978), and Mercure de France (1988).
3 Julian Roberts offers an interesting reading of the character of the intriguer in the context of Benjamin's theory of allegory and the baroque *Trauerspiel* in his book on *Walter Benjamin* (London: Macmillan, 1982), 146.
4 Some excellent studies of Bonnefoy's poetic output and his contribution to the contemporary scene of French letters are John E. Jackson's *Yves Bonnefoy* (Paris: Seghers, 1976), Mary Ann Caws' *Yves Bonnefoy* (Boston: Twayne Publishers, 1984), and Richard Stamelman's "'The Cry that Pierces Music': Yves Bonnefoy" in his book *Lost beyond Telling: Representations of Death and Absence in Modern French Poetry* (Ithaca and London: Cornell University Press, 1990), 122–58.
5 Bonnefoy translated the following Shakespeare plays and narrative poems: *1 Henry IV, Jules César, Hamlet, Le Conte d'hiver, Vénus et Adonis, Le Viol de Lucrèce* (Paris: Club Français du Livre, 1957–60).
6 Jean-Michel Déprats (trans.) *La Tragédie d'Hamlet, Prince de Danemark* (Paris: Granit, 1983), 29.
7 Walter Benjamin's theory of translation is developed in his essay "The Task of the Translator," *Illuminations*, trans. Harry Zohn (New York: Harcourt, Brace & World, 1968), 69–82.
8 ibid., 76.
9 Yves Bonnefoy, "Shakespeare et le poète français," *La Tragédie d'Hamlet* (Paris: Mercure de France, 1962), 229–45; 229.
10 Pierre Leyris and Henri Evans (eds) *Oeuvres complètes de William Shakespeare*, vol. 1 (Paris: Le Club Français du Livre, 1954), various translators.
11 Yves Bonnefoy, "Shakespeare et le poète français," 230.
12 Quoted. in ibid., 231.
13 ibid., 232–3.
14 ibid., 234.
15 ibid.
16 ibid., 233.

17 ibid., 237–8.
18 ibid., 238.
19 ibid., 239.
20 ibid., 240.
21 ibid., 242.
22 ibid., 244.
23 ibid.
24 ibid., 245.
25 In this respect Bonnefoy had already written the following remarks in his 1959 essay, "Shakespeare et le poète français":

> Shakespeare's language is a means, rather than an end; it is always subordinate to the external object, which is something English (but not French) allows. Nouns fade before the real presence of things, which stand starkly before us in the process of becoming. The uninflected adjectives snap quality photographically without raising the metaphysical problem of the relation of quality and substance, as the agreement of adjectives and nouns does in French. English concerns itself naturally with tangible aspects. It accepts the reality of what can be observed and does not admit the possibility of any other kind, of another order of reality; it has a natural affinity with the Aristotelian critique of the Platonic realm of ideas. And even if its Latin roots, to some extent, unsettle this philosophical choice, they do not undermine the natural realism of the language; they simply make it easier to express those moments in life when we are guided by a sense of the ideal."

(I am using John Naughton's translation of this passage in his book *Yves Bonnefoy: The Act and the Place of Poetry* (Chicago and London: University of Chicago Press, 1989), 15.)

26 Yves Bonnefoy, "Shakespeare et le poète français," 252.
27 Leroy C. Breunig, "Bonnefoy's *Hamlet*," *World Literature Today*, 53.3 (1979): 461–5; 463.
28 The Penguin edition of *Hamlet* that I am using is at variance here as regards punctuation. It reads "What a piece of work is a man, ... in form and moving how express and admirable, in action how like an angel" (II, ii, 303–6). Breunig bases his comments on the edition Bonnefoy used, the Dover Wilson edition, which reads "how infinite in faculties, in form and moving, how express and admirable in action, how like an angel in apprehension" (William Shakespeare, *Hamlet*, ed. John Dover Wilson (Cambridge and London: Cambridge University Press, 1936), II, ii, 308–10).
29 Yves Bonnefoy, "Transposer ou traduire *Hamlet*," *La Tragédie d'Hamlet* (Paris: Mercure de France, 1962), 247–56.
30 Christian Pons, "Les traductions de *Hamlet* par des écrivains français," *Etudes Anglaises*, 13.2 (1960): 116–31. Paul Claudel's verset is a lyric line of variable length. Some have likened it to the ancient Greek dithyramb, others have seen in it a certain biblical resonance and power, while still others have seen in it the

influence of Walt Whitman, with whom Claudel was undoubtedly familiar. Claudel himself claimed that the verset originated in his reading of Pascal and Bossuet, in that it does have some elements of the formal liberty of prose.

The basis of the Claudelian verset is not physical. One should rather conceive of it in terms of a psycho-physical breath owing more to religious inspiration than respiration. This is precisely what annoyed Bonnefoy with regard to the verset – its association with religious optimism, more specifically with Catholicism – something which he considers can never be appropriate to Shakespeare.

For a book-length study of Claudel's verset, see Yvette Bozon-Scalzitti's *Le Verset Claudélien* (Paris: Archives des Lettres Modernes, 1965). For a positive evaluation of this form, see Harold A. Waters, *Paul Claudel* (New York: Twayne Publishers, 1970).

31 Yves Bonnefoy, "Transposer ou traduire *Hamlet,*" 247.
32 Walter Benjamin, *The Origin of German Tragic Drama*, trans. John Osborne (London: NLB, 1977), 175.
33 Bonnefoy has taken an inordinate amount of care to be consistent in his word choices as well as in his strategies of compensation. In the second scene of the second act Polonius assures the king that he will find out the truth about Hamlet's madness: "I will find/ Where truth is *hid*, though it were *hid* indeed/ Within the centre" (II, ii, 157–9, emphasis added).

Bonnefoy translates: "et je vais droit/ A la *vérité*, serait-elle (en *vérité!*)/ Cachée au centre de la terre" (p.67, emphasis added).
34 Germaine Marc'hadour, "Woodcock et bécasse: avatars d'une métaphore shakespearienne," *Hamlet Studies*, 6.1–2 (1984): 97–104.
35 ibid., 98.
36 Marc'hadour reviewed twenty-five French translations of these metaphors and it becomes obvious that few of them have kept this repetition. In a note (101n.) she harshly criticizes Gide's translation (1946), of Polonius' line as "Miroir à alouettes!" which he appears to have borrowed from Louis Ménard's 1866 translation ("Quel miroir ou l'on prend l'étourdie alouette!"), and of Laertes' line, "Comme un gibier pris à mon propre piège, Osric," which seems to be Gide's own solution to the problem. Marc'hadour calls Gide's choice of the singular noun "miroir" clumsy, coming as it does after the plural "tous les serments du ciel," and points out that it is quite out of place in this context when the play generally sees "mirror" as a noble metaphor: "hold ... the mirror up to nature" (III, ii, 21–2).

She characterizes the words "gibier" and "piège" as demonstrating great banality. She is surprised that Gide has neglected to preserve the Shakespearian repetition, since he had consulted previous translations which did keep it, and since he did retain the quintuple "tender" in the exchange between Ophelia and Polonius, rendering it by "*offre/ offres/ offres/ offrir.*" He also pointed out the repetition of "fashion" (I, iii, 111–12) in a note.

In fact, only five out of twenty-five translators did retain the double echo and Bonnefoy is praised as one of them. Marc'hadour does not criticize specific words and structures chosen as long as the translator has kept the repetition. Quoting Rainer Pineas she agrees that "the son's echoing of his father's very modes of expression is meant to indicate their identity in all matters." It again underlines "this most dazzling encapsulation of Shakespeare's genius" ("Woodcock et bécasse," 103).
37 ibid., 104.
38 Quoted in ibid., 101. See also Shakespeare's lines I, iii, 114 and V, ii, 300.
39 Yves Bonnefoy, "Transposer ou traduire *Hamlet*," 248.
40 ibid., 247.
41 ibid., 250.
42 *Hamlet*, ed. John Dover Wilson, 222.
43 Benjamin, *Illuminations*, 74–5.
44 Yves Bonnefoy, "Transposer ou traduire *Hamlet*," 251–2.
45 ibid., 253.
46 ibid., 254.
47 ibid., 255.
48 ibid.
49 Walter Benjamin, *The Origin of German Tragic Drama*, 233.
50 Richard Stamelman's article, "The Allegory of Loss and Exile in the Poetry of Yves Bonnefoy," *World Literature Today*, 53.3 (1979): 421–9, caused me to reflect on the link between Walter Benjamin's definition of allegory and Bonnefoy's translation poetics.
51 Yves Bonnefoy, "Comment traduire Shakespeare," *Théâtre/Public*, 44 (1982): 50–5; 50.
52 ibid., 51.
53 ibid., 52.
54 ibid., 52–3.
55 ibid., 53.
56 ibid.
57 Yves Bonnefoy, "Transposer ou traduire *Hamlet*," 251.
58 Quoted in Graham Dunstan Martin, "Bonnefoy's Shakespeare Translations," *World Literature Today*, 53.3 (1979): 465–70; 468. Martin's example roughly corresponds to Hamlet's soliloquy in III, i, 79–80.
59 Rodolphe Gasché, "Saturnine Vision and the Question of Difference: Reflections on Walter Benjamin's Theory of Language," in Rainer Nägele (ed.) *Benjamin's Ground: New Readings of Walter Benjamin* (Detroit: Wayne State University Press, 1988), 83–104; 99–100.
60 Yves Bonnefoy, *Entretiens sur la poésie*, Collection Langages (Neuchâtel: La Baconnière, 1981), 33–4.
61 Yves Bonnefoy, "Comment traduire Shakespeare," 55.
62 Leroy C. Breunig, "Bonnefoy's *Hamlet*," 465.
63 Monique Nemer, "Traduire l'espace," *Théâtre/Public*, 44 (1982): 57–8.

64 ibid, 57.
65 ibid., 58.
66 Yves Bonnefoy, *Rimbaud par lui-même* (Paris: Seuil, 1961), 128.
67 In contrast to several recent representations of *Hamlet*, Chéreau kept to Elizabethan costume (with the exception that the strolling players wore modern dress).
68 Richard Stamelman, "'The Cry that Pierces Music': Yves Bonnefoy," *Lost beyond Telling: Representations of Death and Absence in Modern French Poetry* (Ithaca and London: Cornell University Press, 1990), 131–2.
69 Walter Benjamin, *The Origin of German Tragic Drama*, 232.

6 THEATRE AS TRANSLATION/TRANSLATION AS THEATRE: *SHAKESPEARE'S HAMLET* BY THE THÉÂTRE DU MIROIR

1 Jean-Michel Déprats' unpublished dissertation "Pratique et problématique de la mise en scène shakespearienne contemporaine," Université de Paris VII, 1977, 180–223, describes the three productions in detail.
2 Daniel Mesguich, interview with Gervais Robin, "Un *Hamlet* de plus, entretien avec Daniel Mesguich," *Théâtre/Public*, 18 (1977): 37–40.
3 ibid., 37.
4 These interviews are found in the third issue of *Silex* devoted to *Hamlet*, and several newspaper articles. The special *Silex* issue comprises extracts of Michel Vittoz's translation, a lively conversation between Daniel Mesguich and the interviewers of *Silex*, some of the actors, and two scholars of the University of Bordeaux. "*Hamlet* au centre dramatique national des Alpes," *Silex*, 3 (1977): 7–35, also contains a collage of photos, quotations, and Mesguich's own annotations.
5 Daniel Mesguich, "Un *Hamlet* de plus, entretien avec Daniel Mesguich," 38.
6 ibid., 39.
7 In similar vein, Mesguich says that although he names his company the Théâtre du Miroir and although this was not a gratuitous choice of words on his part, the word *mirror* in itself does not reflect a thing and yet it reflects everything. In his conversation with *Silex*, "*Hamlet* au Centre dramatique national des Alpes," he states that whatever we understand it to mean is true (p.13).
8 ibid.
9 The same can be said of the Schwob–Morand translation (1899) in that its use of language is "artificial."
10 "*Hamlet* au Centre dramatique national des Alpes," 14.
11 Throughout this chapter, I shall be referring to the script of *Hamlet* as performed at the Centre dramatique national des Alpes in Grenoble, in 1977. There are marked differences between the play

script and the printed edition of Vittoz's translation, *Hamlet: Le Livre* (Paris: Editions Papiers/Théâtre, 1986). The printed edition is less experimental and less Lacanian in nature than the script, highlighting in the most vivid terms the distinction between page and stage. References to the script will have "ms" appended to the page number. Translations in square brackets are my own.

12 "*Hamlet* au Centre dramatique national des Alpes," 15–17.
13 In III, iv when Hamlet confronts his mother in her chamber, he enters with the line "Mère, mère, mère" (p.56 ms). The tableau begins with the sound of the sea (*mer*) – waves crash, etc. In his dissertation "Pratique et problématique de la mise en scène shakespearienne," Déprats notes that each scene begins this way (p. 204). The same link between woman and water occurs when Ophelia is drowned.
14 In the original, Hamlet answers Polonius' question, "Will you walk out of the air my Lord?" (II, ii, 206–7), with the retort "Into my grave?" (p.207). Polonius' subsequent reply "Indeed, that's out of the air" (p.208), is rendered into French as "Pour vrai car le mot est bien la mort, sans en avoir l'air [l'r]" (p.32 ms), i.e. the word (*mot*) is indeed death (*mort*) without: (i) seeming to be so (*en avoir l'air*); or (ii) without the "r" (*l'r*, pronounced *l'air*).
15 As Mesguich says in his interview with Robin, "c'est en lisant son être que l'acteur s'écrit" [in reading their "being" actors write themselves]. Daniel Mesguich, "Un *Hamlet* de plus, entretien avec Daniel Mesguich," 40.
16 "*Hamlet* au Centre dramatique national des Alpes," 26.
17 ibid., 30.
18 In a personal interview, Jean-Michel Déprats told me that the original 1977 Grenoble production had the three walls of the Italian stage tiled with mirrors, so that all characters were decomposed in reflection.
19 Judith Gershman, "Daniel Mesguich's *Shakespeare's Hamlet*," *The Drama Review*, 25.2 (1981): 19.
20 "*Hamlet* au Centre dramatique national des Alpes," 31; Judith Gershman, "Daniel Mesguich's *Shakespeare's Hamlet*," 19–20.
21 I am indebted to Vivian Eden's insights on translation as theatre and game as expounded in her dissertation, "An Examination of How Translation Is Like Theatre with an Annotated Translation from the Hebrew of the Novel *The Flying Camel and the Golden Hump* by Aharon Megged and an Introduction to the Novel," University of Iowa, 1986.
22 "*Hamlet* au Centre dramatique national des Alpes," 18.
23 See Vivian Eden, "An Examination of How Translation Is Like Theatre with an Annotated Translation from the Hebrew of the Novel *The Flying Camel and the Golden Hump* by Aharon Megged and an Introduction to the Novel," 331.
24 Yorick features neither in the published translation nor in the manuscript I have, but Jean-Michel Déprats ("Pratique et problématique de la mise en scène shakespearienne," 207) and Judith

Gershman ("Daniel Mesguich's Shakespeare's Hamlet," 25) report that in the production they saw, Yorick impersonates both the gravedigger and Hamlet, speaking gibberish in these roles.

25 See Jean-Michel Déprats, "Pratique et problématique de la mise en scène shakespearienne," 207.
26 Hélène Cixous, "Un Fils," *Hamlet: Le Livre* (Paris: Editions Papiers/ Théâtre, 1986), 9–15. Part of this text is published along with Vittoz's translation, as an introductory article ("Un Fils") which does not form part of the published translation of the play.
27 I am once again indebted to Judith Gershman's eyewitness account of the original production (1977) which provides additional information not contained in the script of that production. Interestingly enough Vittoz's published translation does not have a single "foreign" word with the exception of Ophelia's line: "For bonnie sweet robin is all my joy" (p.141) taken directly from IV, v, 187 of Shakespeare.
28 Judith Gershman, "Daniel Mesguich's *Shakespeare's Hamlet*," 27–8.

Index

abstractions in Gide 87
Académie Française and Ducis 29, 36
acculturation of *Hamlet* 75–6
action filtered through language 33, 35
action and inaction 59
additions by Gide 83–4
adjectives: adverbial 72; and nouns 101
adverbial adjectives 72
adverbial phrases 72
alexandrines 96, 112, 113, 114; Ducis 4, 33; Dumas 52, 55; Hugo 47
allegory, *Hamlet* as 80, 87, 92–121
alliteration 71
allusions 75
ambiguity in Shakespeare 94, 103
animal imagery 89, 103–4
applied linguistics and translation 1, 3
archaisms: Gide 87; Schwob/Morand 66, 68–9, 73, 82, 87
Aristotelianism of English language 99, 102, 107
articles (parts of speech) 72, 73
assonance 71
audience and translations 3, 24
aural language in translations 3, 73–4

Bailey, Helen Phelps 36–7
balance 32
ballads, French 75–6

Barrault, Jean-Louis 79–81, 82, 83, 88, 91
Bautista/Baptista 57
Beaugrande, Robert de 14–15
Belleforest, François de 64
Benjamin, Walter 94, 97, 103, 108, 109, 114
Bernardo: Mesguich/Vittoz 131; Schwob/Morand 71
Bernhardt, Sarah 4, 58, 61–2
Bladé 64–5
blank verse in French 4–5
Bonnefoy, Yves 82, 83, 92–121, 138
bourgeois values 17–19; Ducis 36–41
Breunig, Leroy 101

cadence of *Hamlet* 88–9
Cairns, Nancy Lee 91
canons of literature 6–7, 8, 21, 23, 60
capitalist society and translation 5, 17–19
Captain, the 56
Catullus 66–7
chaos in *Hamlet* 109
Châtelain, Chevalier de 112–13
Chéreau, Patrice 92, 118–19
Cixous, Hélène 135
Claretie 57–8, 60
clarity of translation 82
classicism: French 96, 100; of Gide 87; *see also* neoclassicism
Claudel, Paul 108, 159–60

Claudius: Bonnefoy 106, 107, 117; Ducis 31, 32, 33, 36, 37; Dumas/Meurice 49, 50, 51, 54, 56; Gide 86; Mesguich/Vittoz 127–8; Schwob/Morand 73
code-abiding process, translation as 5, 17–18, 41
codes 5–7; linguistic 73; master 6, 19–20
colloquialisms 33, 69, 88
colonialism and translation 5–6, 18–19
Comédie Française 4; and Ducis 28–9, 35, 36, 41, 42–3; and Dumas 45, 47; and Meurice 57, 58; neoclassicism 45, 47–8, 60; and Schwob/Morand 60
comic interludes 31, 53; *see also* gravediggers
communication, translation as 12–13, 15–17, 21
comparative linguistics and translation 1
consistency in translations 3
consumability 17–19
contemporaneity of language 68–9, 86–7
content and form 83, 108, 110
contextual consistency in translations 3
contrastive linguistics and translation 1
criticism of translations 2, 3, 22
cultural *see* socio-cultural

Dargan, E. Preston 36
decentering, poetics of 120
decision process, translation as 15–17, 20, 24
decolonisation and translation 5–6, 18–19
deletions: by Bonnefoy 107; by Gide 83–4
dénouement *see* finale
Déprats, Jean-Michel 93
Diderot, Denis 35
doublets in Shakespeare 71, 73, 84, 85, 101–2, 103

Douma, Felix 146
Dover Wilson, John 93, 94, 106
Dowden, Edward 67
duality in Shakespeare 33, 105
Ducis, Jean-François 4, 5, 26–44, 46, 63, 65, 95, 96, 138
Duflos, Raphaël 57
Dumas, Alexandre, *père* 45–60, 63, 65, 95, 138
Dumas, Alexandre, *fils* 58
dynamic equivalence in translations 3

egalitarianism in language 74
elitism of French language 74
Elizabethan stage 111, 116
ellipsis, Shakespeare's 72, 73, 116
Elvire 31, 33
emblematic nouns 102
English language: Aristotelianism of 99; compared with French 94, 98, 99, 102
English verse, compared with French 67, 82, 88, 110, 112, 114
epithets in Shakespeare 73
être/to be 72–3
Even-Zohar, Itamar 5, 6–10, 14, 20, 23, 147
exclusivity of French poetry 98, 102
existential Hamlet 80
exoticizing translation 16–17, 76

Falstaff 97
family values and Ducis 36–41
Fedorov, Andrei 1
filial piety of Hamlet 36–8, 40
finale to *Hamlet* in Dumas/Meurice 54–5, 56
Florenne, Yves 157
fluency in translation 17–19, 24
folklore, French 5, 64–5
form and content 83, 108, 110
formal correspondence in translations 3
formal languages 13

Fortinbras: Dumas/Meurice 46, 56–7, 59; Gide 79, 85, 91
free verse 113, 114–15
French ballads 75–6
French classicism 96
French folklore 5, 64–5, 75–6
French language: and blank verse 4–6; compared with English 94, 98, 99, 102; elitism 74; gender 100–1; modern 82; Platonism of 99; *see also* archaisms
French prosody 63, 82, 96, 98, 100
French romanticism *see* romanticism
French sources of *Hamlet* 64–5, 75–6
French verse compared with English 67, 82, 88, 110, 112, 114
functionalist approaches to translation 10

game, translation as 15
Gautier, Théophile 55
gender in French language 100–1
Gershman, Judith 131, 164
Gertrude: Bonnefoy 104, 106–7; Ducis 31, 32, 33, 36, 39–40; Dumas/Meurice 49, 53, 54–5; Gide 88–9
"Get thee to a nunnery" in Dumas/Meurice 59
Ghost: Bonnefoy 94, 119; Ducis 27, 30, 31–2, 38, 44; Dumas/Meurice 49, 50, 53–5, 56, 57, 58; Mesguich/Vittoz 130–1, 132
Gide, André 77–91, 97, 138
"globe" 87
goal-oriented activity, translation as 5, 20, 24
Goethe, J.W. von 150
gongorism 65–6
Gonzago 51, 58
gravediggers' scene: Bonnefoy 119; Ducis 30, 31; Dumas/Meurice 53, 56

Guildenstern: Ducis 31; Dumas/Meurice 53; Gide 85

Hamlet: Bonnefoy 93, 96, 105, 107, 111, 117, 119–20; Ducis 31–5, 36, 37–42, 44; Dumas/Meurice 46–7, 49, 50–1, 52–3, 56–9; Gide 80, 84–7, 88, 89, 90; Mesguich/Vittoz 128, 135; Schwob/Morand 71, 73, 74–5
Harlow, Barbara 5, 18–19
Hecuba: Dumas/Meurice 50, 58; Gide 86
hendecasyllables 113–14
historicizing translation 16–17, 66–9, 76
Holmes, James S 5, 14, 17, 148–9
Holub, Robert 147
honour 96
hope and *Hamlet* 88
Horatio: Bonnefoy 94, 107; Ducis 31; Dumas/Meurice 50, 51, 56, 59; Gide 84–5; Mesguich/Vittoz 126, 131; Schwob/Morand 71, 73
Hugo, François-Victor 59, 97, 117
Hugo, Victor 45, 46, 47, 55

imagery, animal 89, 103–4
imperialism and translation 5–6, 18–19
inclusivity of English poetry 98, 102
individualism 17–19
intelligible *Hamlet* 83
invisibility of translator 17

Jacquot, Jean 152–3
Jameson, Fredric 6, 19–20
Jauss, Hans Robert 22, 147
Jenkins, Harold 93, 94
Judith, Mme 61
Justice: Fortinbras as 91

Kean, Edmund 45
Kemble, Charles 45, 46, 51
La Place, Antoine de 26–8

Laertes: Bonnefoy 104, 119;
  Ducis 31, 32; Dumas/Meurice
  49, 50, 51, 53, 54, 56, 58
Lamord 86
language: and action 33, 35;
  elitism 74; metaphysical
  differences 94; pure 95; *see
  also* English; French
Le Tourneur, P. 33
Lefevere, André 6, 19–20, 146,
  147–8, 150
Levý, Jiří 5, 15–17, 149
linguistic codes 73
linguistics and translation 1
literal translation: Bonnefoy
  109; Gide 111; Schwob/
  Morand 67–8
literature: codes in 5–7;
  stratification in 7–10
love 96
Lucianus 51

Macready, William 46, 51
Mallarmé, Stéphane 101
manipulation, literature as 18–20
mapping in translation 5, 13–14
Marcellus: Bonnefoy 94;
  Mesguich/Vittoz 131; Schwob/
  Morand 73
Marc'hadour, Germaine 103–4,
  160–1
Martin, Graham Dunstan 112
master codes 6, 19–20
matricial norms 10–14; Ducis 30,
  42; Dumas/Meurice 49
meaning in *Hamlet* 105, 108, 109
melancholy of Hamlet 105
melodrama: Dumas 48, 49, 53,
  55–6, 60; Hugo 47
Mesguich, Daniel 122–36, 137,
  138
metaphysical differences
  between French and English
  94, 98, 99
Meurice, Paul 45–60
modern French 82
modernizing translation 16–17,
  82–3, 86–7
monologues of Hamlet 109
moralizing elements in *Hamlet* 36
Morand, Eugène 4–5, 60, 61–76,
  138
Mounet-Sully 57, 59, 60
"Mourir, dormir ..." *see* "To die
  ..."
Mousetrap *see* play within the
  play
Musset, Alfred de: *Lorenzaccio* 62

naturalizing translation 16–17,
  75–6, 81–2
negotiation, translation as
  12–13, 20–1, 23
Nemer, Monique 115–17
neoclassicism: Comédie
  Française 45, 47–8, 60; Ducis
  29–30, 33, 36–7, 41, 46; *see also*
  classicism
neologisms in Schwob/Morand
  66
Nida, Eugene 1, 3
Noël, Jean-Claude 68, 84, 88–9
non-canonized literature 6–7, 41
Norceste 31, 32, 38, 40
normative approaches to
  translation 3, 4, 10, 16, 21,
  24–5
norms in translation 10–14, 82
Norway: Dumas/Meurice 46, 56,
  58, 59; Gide 85, 87
noun phrases in Shakespeare 85
nouns: and adjectives 101;
  emblematic 102; plural 101

obligatory shifts in translation 13
Old French 68–9, 71–2, 76
operational norms in translation
  10–14
Ophelia: Bonnefoy 96, 106;
  Ducis 30, 31, 32, 33, 36, 41;
  Dumas/Meurice 47, 50, 51–3,
  58, 59; Gide 89–90; Mesguich/
  Vittoz 134–5; Schwob/Morand
  70–1
optional shifts in translation 13
oral language in translations 3
participles, present 101
peace and Fortinbras 79

pentameter in *Hamlet* 108, 112
Perrin, Emile 57
personal pronouns 100–1
personification 72, 75
Platonism of French language 99
play within the play 47, 51, 65, 85, 89
playable *Hamlet* 83, 88
pleonasms in Shakespeare 84
plurals 101
poetics 11, 111–12; of decentering 120
Pollock, Juliet 152–3
Polonius: Bonnefoy 92, 104, 119; Ducis 31, 33; Dumas/Meurice 50, 51, 56, 58, 59; Gide 89, 90; Mesguich/Vittoz 129; Schwob/Morand 73
polysystem, literature as 5, 6–10, 21, 23
Pons, Christian 102, 105
Pourtalès, Guy de 80
power relations with Comédie Française 47, 60
preliminary norms in translation 10–14
prescriptive theories of translation 3–4
present participles 101
Priam 58
primary literature 7–10, 23
priorities in translation 3
pronouns, personal 100–1
prose versions of *Hamlet* 4, 61, 63, 82–3, 97, 110
prosody: French 63, 82, 96, 98, 100; Shakespeare's 108, 110, 112–13
punning in Shakespeare 33, 74, 93

questions in *Hamlet* 109

Racine, Jean 98
readability of translation 17–19, 24, 73
rebus, translation as 5
redundancy in Shakespeare 83, 84, 107

referentiality, Shakespeare's 69, 103, 118
regular verse 112
relevance of *Hamlet* 81–2
repetition in Shakespeare 83, 103
resistance, translation as 5–6, 18–19
"the rest is silence": Dumas/Meurice 58
rewriting, translation as 6
rhythms of *Hamlet* 88–9, 90, 100, 103, 108, 114–15
Roberts, Julian 158
Robin, Gervais 123
romanticism: Comédie Française 45; Dumas 47, 53, 55–6; French 96–7
Rosencrantz: Ducis 31; Dumas/Meurice 59; Gide 85
Rouvière 49

Schwob, Marcel 4–5, 60, 61–76, 84, 87, 138
secondary literature 7–10
semiotics of literature 6–7
sensibility of Hamlet 36–7
shifts in translation 5, 13, 20
Smith, Christopher 62
social function of theatre 81
socio-cultural influences on translation 4–25
source text oriented translation 62–3
spatial dimensions of *Hamlet* 111, 115–17, 118–19
Stackelberg, Jürgen von 36
stage, Elizabethan 111
staging: by Chéreau 118–19; by Mesguich 122–36, 137, 138
Stamelman, Richard 120
Stendhal 45–6
stratification in literature 7–10
symmetry 32
syntax, Shakespeare's 72, 73
system, literature as 5, 6–10
Taber, Charles 3
Talma 38, 41–4, 60
tautology in Shakespeare 83, 84, 107

teleology of translation 16–17
textual norms in translation 10–14
Théâtre du Miroir 122–36, 137
theatre, social function of 81, 91
time-dependent influences on translation 4–5, 6, 8, 17, 22, 24, 68–9
to be/être 72–3
"To be or not to be": Bonnefoy/Chéreau 112–13, 117, 119; Châtelain 112–13; Ducis 32, 33–5, 38, 42; Voltaire 96
"To die, to sleep ...": Bonnefoy 117; Ducis 42
Tourey, Gideon 5, 10–14, 147–8
tragedy, classical 30–1, 41
transcoding 20
transformative process, translation as 16–17
transliteration 109; Schwob/Morand 71
triplets in Shakespeare 71
Tytler, Alexander 2

urn in Ducis 32–3, 35, 38, 40, 49

van Tieghem, Philippe 63
Vanderauwera, Ria 147–8

Venuti, Lawrence 5, 17–19, 146
verbal consistency in translations 3
verse: free 113; French compared with English 67, 82, 88, 110, 112, 114; regular 112
verse form, Shakespeare's 108, 110, 112
versets 108, 112
Vittoz, Michel 126–36, 137, 138
Voltaire 27–8, 30–1, 96
Voltimand: Ducis 31; Dumas/Meurice 56
vulgar language 33, 69, 88

wartime France: and Gide/Barrault 79–82, 87
"What a piece of work ..." in Bonnefoy 120
Wilson, John Dover 93, 94, 106
women actors 60
word order and Schwob/Morand 71
written language in translations 3

Yorick scene: Bonnefoy 119; Ducis 30; Dumas/Meurice 56; Mesguich/Vittoz 134

ted in the USA/Agawam, MA
ruary 2, 2015

7620.016